Empty Souls Living Beyond Your Grave

I0529035

Juanita R. Vedder

Quantum Discovery
A LITERARY AGENCY

ISBN
978-1-963254-05-1 (Paperback)
978-1-963254-06-8 (eBook)

TABLE OF CONTENTS

PREFACE

My name is Juanita R. Vedder, and I am a Christian, totally dedicated to my Lord. I have dealt with some serious issues in my life that has nearly caused me to end my own life. The pain of one's soul runs so deep that it cuts like a knife, hoping to find some way to end it all, and to think that the only way to end it all is through death. But in reality, death only inflicts more pain, the kind of pain that God says will never end. And that is living in hell for all eternity. There is no escaping eternity, and there is no way of escaping death. The second your destiny has been chosen by you, you will remain there, and there will be no chance to change your mind and come back to earth to make a new start to make things better. You must choose to make things better now. You have one life to live, so you need to make the best of it with what you have.

At one point in my life, I was contemplating suicide. I did not want to actually die; I just wanted my pain to go away. But the only way to end my pain I thought was to die. That is until God got a hold on me, hugged me, and said to me suicide is not an option for me. The touch of God's hand is so awesome, and God loves me so much that I will never contemplate suicide again. God has turned what was meant for evil to the good. I now live for God, and I walk in His ways. I pray that God uses this book to reach out to others who are contemplating suicide. Though this world is so full of evil and hate, so much love and good will come from it if we turn to God and use our pain as a stepping stone instead of the weight that pulls you down in life. My friend, *death* is not the answer to life's problems. Our days here on earth are numbered, so please let God call your number before you decide to take it. For God says that one day He will wipe away every tear and we shall feel no more pain.

Revelation 21:4 says, "God will wipe away every tear from their eyes, there shall be no more death, nor sorrow, nor crying. There shall be no more pain, for the former things have passed away." God is with us. He did not abandon this world, therefore, we shouldn't either. For God will call us home one day. So let that day be for God to take.

Please, my dearest friend, turn to God for comfort and let Him take control of your life. Hell is certainly not the place to be for your soul to have to suffer for eternity. God also makes it very clear in His word that you are awake after you die. Our body is just a shell that carries our spirit. And when the body dies, it just goes back to the ground and turns to dust, and the spirit departs from the body. And believe it or not, your soul is awake after it leaves the body, and I know this, for the Bible tells me so in Luke 16:19–31.

INTRODUCTION

Warning: This book contains intense and disturbing contents. Viewer discretion is advised. This book is not intended for younger children. Please be advised when reading this book that you keep an open mind to the reality of life and death in general. This book may or may not be appropriate or suitable for you. The contents of this book are truly based upon biblical knowledge. There are two chapters that may intimidate you, "The Devil's Child" and "The Reality of Your Conscience." I have personally spent many hours studying specific scriptures relating to life and death, heaven and hell. I have also spent many hours researching all the information needed to write this book. In regards to reading this book, I would like to advise you to have a Bible and a commentary at hand for the research I have provided.

This book is based upon facts about life and death, heaven and hell, and where do we go once, we pass from this life into the next. Do you believe in life after death? Do you believe in heaven and hell? Do you believe that your eternal existence will become your final destiny? As to those who contemplate suicide or if you know of someone who is, then please read this book! I truly believe this book will help you understand the meaning and purpose of life and therefore save a life that is worth living. All life is worth living!

Many people go to their early grave because they lack the knowledge for living a bountiful life in an evil and chaotic world. People also lack the understanding that death is the final answer to all of their problems, their pain and agony, all of their shame and guilt, or whatever it is that is causing them to contemplate suicide. People mainly lack the understanding that their life is not theirs to take. Yes, they may have the power to end their life, but they do not have that right. God did not give us that right to end our own life or take the life of another.

There was a time in my life that I wanted to end all of my pain and agony, but I didn't want to die! I'm not talking about physical pain; my pain was beyond comprehension. I knew God's word about committing murder. Suicide is murder against oneself. I knew I would end up in hell if I would have committed suicide. This is why writing this book is so important to me. If the truth of God's word saved me from hell, then I know it will save you, I believe. We must go through pain, trials, and hardships in order to have a better future.

God is the one who created all living and breathing creatures, and I truly believe that it should be God who takes our last breath. People need to think outside the box and realize that they do have a future in the next life to come; it's called eternity, whether it is in heaven or in hell. This is what eternity is like. People will be awake. Though the body dies, the spirit remains awake. People will have a conscience, and they will know what is going on. The spirit will not sleep or rest. People will remember how they lived out their life on earth, whether it is good or bad. People can communicate with one another in heaven and hell. The sad part is the people who end up in hell will have no mercy for their soul. There will be no escaping from hell, and your soul will be tormented forever and ever. Read Luke 16:19–31; it is about Lazarus and the rich man! So just remember that when you make that final choice to end your life, there will be no turning back and asking God to give you another chance to make things right with Him, and there will be no forgiveness for what you have done. People often make the mistake of thinking that if they ask God to forgive them before they end their life, that God would still forgive them and take them to heaven with Him. Not so. God will not forgive anyone who intentionally destroys what He has created, someone who purposely goes against His will and His commandments under the assumption that they knew what they were doing is wrong. That would be like stealing and then asking the judge to forgive you and not punish you for your crime.

Wrong choices have consequences. God is no respecter of persons, and God does not have favorites. People need to be aware of their afterlife and the consequences they will have to face.

Many parents lack the knowledge to teach their children about the horrible consequences when contemplating suicide. People need to be warned about the consequences of premature death. In God's word, Hosea 4:6 says, "My people are destroyed for lack of knowledge." So, if only in the Lord do, we find life, then we better make it our number one priority to learn as much about God and his ways as much as possible; even some knowledge is useful.

I assume that there would be fewer suicides if more preachers would teach knowledge on this subject about life and death and the afterlife of heaven and hell. There are so many different religions and churches that no one knows who or what church to believe. One thing that is for sure is that not many churches, if any, preaches on the afterlife. I wonder why. This should be top priority for people to know especially our younger generation! I believe that there would be less gang violence and less hate crimes if people had knowledge of their actions and what eternal punishment they would have to look forward to. It's time for people to take heed to God's warnings now, for tomorrow may never come. I do hope and pray that you consider reading the rest of this book.

PROLOGUE

What is it that people *expect* to accomplish by taking their own lives? Is death the greatest achievement that anyone has ever accomplished? Life here on earth is very shortly lived compared to eternity! People say that life on earth is hell that we face every day, because life is so full of pain, sorrow, heartache, evil, violence, and so full of hate that there seems to be no joy, love, peace, or happiness. But why is that?

Evil seems to be taking over the world, and only a few will find true joy and happiness in this chaotic world. Who are the lucky ones that seem to have this so-called love and peace in this world of hell that we are living in? It is the ones who are called to live by God's word! So that means that this should include every living human being, right? But, unfortunately, only so many people will choose to obey God and live by his word.

As we stumble and journey through life, time goes on, as we keep searching for the right answer to life's problems. I heard the saying, "People are not born with directions on how to take care of the baby." Well, that's not true. We have the word of God who tells us how to raise our children. Read Proverbs 22:6. God explains the blueprint for all humanity.

1

An Empty Soul

An empty soul, what is the meaning of it? How does a person's soul become empty, and why is it empty? This is a question many are curious about, including me. I once had an empty soul until I acknowledged God and was baptized, and now my soul is no longer empty but filled with the love of God and His grace for me.

An empty soul refers to a person's soul that is empty. The human soul pertains to the mind, will, and emotions. Have you experienced that feeling of emptiness, the feeling of something is missing in your life but you can't seem to pinpoint what it is that is making you feel this way? Well, this is the purpose why I have written this book, but I would not have been able to write this book without the help of God and His precious Son, Jesus Christ. It is to them I give all credit to.

2

Born into Sin

Before any human being existed, the world was perfectly created just the way God had planned it. Sin did not exist until after Adam and Eve disobeyed God when they were in the garden of Eden. Sin and corruption entered into existence after Adam and Eve ate the apple from the tree of knowledge of good and evil. Go back to the very beginning of human life when God first created man, which is Adam. Let's look at the scriptures taken from the beginning of the Bible, starting with the book of Genesis!

"The Lord God formed man of the dust of the ground, and breathed into his nostrils the breath of life; and man became a living soul" (Genesis 2:7). At this time and point in life, man was not born physically from a woman's physical body. And no one existed yet but Adam. Now read Genesis 2:21, 22, and 23.

And the Lord God caused a deep sleep to fall upon Adam, and he slept; and he [God] took one of his ribs [Adam's] and closed up the flesh instead thereof. (Gen. 2:21)

And the rib which the Lord God had taken from man, made he a woman [Eve] and brought her unto the man. (Gen. 2:22)

And Adam said, this is now bone of my bone and flesh of my flesh; she shall be called woman, because she was taken out of man. (Genesis. 2:21-23)

Notice that neither was the woman born from a physical body. She was taken from man's rib. Still, at this time, no one was born into the world yet. And God's earth is still perfect and sinless. So, when did sin enter the earth, and when did God curse the ground? Read Genesis 2:16 and 17. The tree of knowledge of good and evil!

And the Lord God commanded the man saying, of every tree of the garden thou mayest freely eat; but of the tree of the knowledge of good and evil, thou shall not eat of it; for in that day that thou eatest thou shalt surely die. (Genesis 2:16-17)

Disobedience is what opened the door for sin to enter into this chaotic world. The devil now rules the earth and every human that will be born of a physical body, the woman. Here are more scriptures.

For God doth know that in the day that ye eat thereof, then your eyes shall be opened, and ye shall be as gods, knowing good and evil. And when the woman saw that the tree was good for food, and that it was pleasant to the eyes, and a tree to be desired to make one wise, she took of the fruit thereof and did eat, and gave also unto her husband [Adam] with her, and he did eat. (Genesis 3:5-6)

And unto Adam he said, because you hast harkened unto the voice of thy wife, and hast eaten of the tree, of which I commanded thee, saying, thou shalt not eat of it; cursed is the ground for thy sake; in sorrow thou shalt eat of it all the days of thy life. (Genesis 3:17)

The severe punishment that was sent upon man and woman, as well as the sin that affected nature, was meant to remind all mankind that of the devastating consequences of their sin will make them to become dependent on God. In this world, life is not perfect and is perverted. Human judgment that oftentimes decides what is good and what is evil. But this was not God's original plan.

You see, God's plan was for mankind to only know what is good and not to know any evil. And God's original plan was for humans to depend only on Him and His ord. Life was not meant for us to live apart from God. When Adam and Eve sinned against God, moral and spiritual death came immediately. Moral death consists in the death of God's life in Him and their nature becoming sinful, and spiritual death meant that their former relationship with God was destroyed. Now since the sin of Adam and Eve, every person born comes into the world with a sinful nature. This corruption of human nature involves the desire to go one's selfish ways without the concern for God or even the concern for others. This is passed on to every child born into sin. Adam introduced the law of sin and death to the whole human race. Adam and Eve are the reason why every human born into sin are separated from God. Read Romans.

Wherefore, as by one man sin entered into the world. and death by sin; and death passed upon all men, for that all have sinned. (Romans 5:12)

So, there were two results that followed when Adam sinned against God: sin and corruption! Now all humans are born with a selfish impulse to commit sin. Sin is the desire of the human heart. Now check out these scriptures.

And the eyes of them both were opened, and they knew that they were naked, and they sewed fig leaves together and made themselves aprons. (Genesis 3:7)

Now this next verse indicates that the first human that is born will be born into sin. And up until now, no humans were born yet.

Unto the woman he said, I will greatly multiply thy sorrow and thy conception; in sorrow thou shalt bring forth children; and thy desire shall be to thy husband, and he shall rule over thee. (Genesis 3:16)

Now starting in chapter 4 of the book of Genesis, Eve is the very first human to give birth, to the first baby born into sin. I would say woman, but too many children and teenagers are having babies. Eve gave birth to the first man born, and his name was Cain. Yes, sin is now born into all human beings. Sin entered the earth through Adam, but sin was born through Cain. There are two words here that make all the difference: *entered* and *born*. Sin entered before it became born to all humans.

Now Eve gave birth to her second child named Abel! So, let's clarify this. Adam was the first human being created, but Cain was the first human being born. You see, Adam was not born, for he was created, and Eve was not born either; she was taken from Adam's rib. Pretty amazing it is to know how God has everything all planned out from the beginning of time!

So, as I get into this next chapter about birth and sin, I will speak about how old one must one be that God would hold accountable for their sins.

3

The Devil's Child

Note: As you read this chapter, there may be some matters that may cause an issue to how you believe. But you need to know that these verses are from the Bible, and whether you believe it to be true or not does not change what God says. Please be advised that you may not like what you read! But please don't stop reading, for it could save your life and change the way you live, and hopefully for the better! May the good Lord help you as you read this chapter.

Yes, that is right, the devil has children too. As a matter of fact, every child born into this world starts off being the devil's child. Wow, that can be very devastating to believe, but it is the truth. As a baby grows, they believe the devil's lies and carries out his purpose of defying God; they deny the divinity and the work of Christ, and they do not care that sin is highly offensive to God. They live their lives as they are taught. Every human being is born into sin. Here is what God says about physical birth.

The earth was also corrupt before God, and the earth was filled with violence. So, God looked upon the earth, and indeed it was corrupt; for all flesh have corrupted their way on the earth.
(Genesis. 282 6:11-12)

Therefore, just as one-man sin entered the world, and death through sin, and thus death spread to all men, because all sinned. (Romans 5:12)

He that committeth sin is of the devil; for the devil sinneth from the beginning. (1 John 3:8)

Yet man is born to trouble, as the sparks fly upward. (Job 5:7)

Man, who is born of woman is a few days and full of trouble. (Job 14:1)

Does God condemn humans for being born sinners or just only for the sins they commit? Every human being lives and remains in sin until the day they get saved, and then they will become a child of God. Now as I had mentioned in my previous chapter, sin was not originally part of God's plan for the human race. So, what shall one do to return to God's original plan? We must acknowledge and believe that there is a God, and then we must confess our sins and confess that Jesus Christ is Lord and Savior of the universe. One must also believe that Jesus Christ is the Son of the living God.

My son, if thou wilt receive my words and hide my commandments with thee; So that thou incline thy ear unto wisdom, and apply thine heart to understanding; Yes, if you criest after knowledge, and liftest up thy voice for understanding; If thou seekest her as silver and searchest for her as for hidden treasures; Then shalt thou understand the fear of the Lord, and find the knowledge of God. For the Lord giveth wisdom: out of his mouth cometh knowledge and understanding. (Proverbs. 2:1-6)

Jesus answered and said to him, most assuredly, I say to you, Unless one is born again, he cannot see the kingdom of God. (John 3:3)

That which is born of flesh is flesh, and that which is born of spirit is spirit. (John 3:6)

Having been born again, not of corruptible seed but incorruptible, through the word of God which lives and abides forever. (1 Peter. 1:23)

So here you have two sets of children. There is the devil's child, the evil one; and there is God's child, the good one. The devil's child is a sinner, and God's child is a saint, but a saint still sins. A saint is covered from their sins by the grace of God and the blood of the Lamb, which is Jesus Christ. As you may wonder what it means by Jesus Christ being the Lamb of God, here are a few scriptures on that. Jesus, the Lamb of God, who takes away the sins of this world.

Behold, the Lamb of God, which taketh away the sins of the world. (John 1:29)

Jesus is the Lamb of God that God provided to be sacrificed in the place of sinners. By His death, Jesus made provision for the removal of the guilt and power of sin, and Jesus opened the way to God for us all.

In the Old Testament times, an actual lamb was used for the sacrificing of sins. See the scripture:

And they shall take of the blood, and strike it on the two side posts and on the upper door of the houses. (Exodus 12:7)

And the blood shall be to you for a token upon the houses where ye are; and when I see the blood [God] I will pass over you and the plague shall not be upon you to destroy you. (Exodus 12:13)

The Passover lamb and its blood represents Jesus Christ's blood as the Lamb of God which taketh away the sins of the world. In these days that we live in now, we no longer need a lamb to sacrifice to take away our sins. Through our faith in Jesus Christ, our sins are forgiven. Amen to that Here is one more scripture.

But with the precious blood of Christ, as of a lamb without blemish and without spot. (1 Peter 1:19)

8

The scriptures plainly set-forth the sacrificial death of Christ on the cross as that which procures the believer's redemption. A believer is released from bondage and slavery to sin. Just remember that it is only God that can make us righteous, and we cannot and will not save ourselves from the sins of this world and definitely cannot save ourselves from going to hell. But we can certainly put ourselves there!

God loves every human born of flesh very much, but unfortunately, God gave us a free living will to choose Him or the devil.

I call heaven and earth to record this day against you that I have set before your life and death, blessing and cursing: therefore, choose life that both thou and thy seed may live. (Deuteronomy 30:19)

Which one are you choosing? Life means living in obedience to God's will and do what is good! Death means disobedience, and doing what the devil wants you to do, which are the bad things. But if you do not know Christ, then doing what is bad may seem good to you. When God speaks of life and death, He is referring to the spiritual nature. The physical body is not the only thing that will live or die!

Now not every human born into this world will have that chance to make that choice. Some babies die before birth or even after birth! So, then you may wonder, *how old does a person have to be to make that type of a serious choice?* To answer your thought, there is no scripture that gives a certain age limit. Okay. So, then you may wonder about babies who know no different, since they are not born pure and are sinners, will they go to hell when they die?

Remember, God does not send people to hell; we send ourselves there by not choosing Jesus Christ and obeying the word of God and get baptized. Babies cannot be baptized by being submerged underwater because they do not know what sin is. But God did say that when one is knowledgeable of their sins and knows right from wrong, then they are old enough to make their choice of which one to serve, the devil or God. Now how old does a person have to be before they are able to acknowledge right from wrong and the commandments of God? How old must one be to be saved from their sins? How old is old enough to understand knowledge? And how old was Adam and Eve when God gave them knowledge of the tree? And how old were they when they acknowledged their sin when they ate from the apple and their eyes became open to knowledge of their sins? I have not personally found any scriptures that speak of a certain age limit! Here are some scriptures that talk about knowledge.

Moreover, your little ones, which ye said should be a prey, and your children which in that day had no knowledge between good and evil, they shall go in there, and unto them will I give it, and they shall possess it. (Deuteronomy 1:39)

Whom shall he teach knowledge? and whom shall he make to understand doctrine? them that are weaned from the milk and drawn from the breast. (Isaiah 28:9)

I find this scripture a clue to one's age of knowledge. In the *Matthew Henry's Commentary*, the scripture is explained.

The prophet complains of the wretched stupidity of the people, that they were unteachable. Their prophets and ministers were designed to teach the knowledge of God and His will, and to make them understand doctrine. This is God's way of dealing with men, to enlighten men's minds first with the knowledge of His truth, and thus to gain their affections, and bring their wills into a compliance with His laws. They left no means untried to do them good but taught them as *little children* that are beginning to learn that are taken from the breast to the book. For among the Jews, it was common for mothers to nurse their children until they were three years old and almost ready for school. They teach them, as they are capable, the good knowledge of the Lord and to instruct them even when they are but newly weaned from milk. They have been taught, as children are taught to read, by precept upon precept and taught to write line upon line, a little here and a little there, a little of one thing and a little of another, that instructions might be pleasing, a little at one time and a little at another, that they might not have their memories overcharged, a little from one prophet and a little from another. Teachers should accommodate themselves to the capacity of the learners and give them what they most need a little at a time. Now this next verse is based upon fear for God. Do little children fear God?

The fear of the Lord is the beginning of knowledge; but fools despise wisdom and instruction. (Proverbs 1:7)

The fear of the Lord!

This type of fear that God speaks about is not the way the world thinks about fear! To fear God is like a reverence, awe for God and His power, majesty, and holiness that produces in us a fear of sinning against Him. Such reverence is essential to gaining a heart for God's wisdom on a daily basis.

The world today as we know it has no fear for God. Just look at all of the violence going on in the world, including drugs, alcohol, sexual impurity, adultery and people divorcing, murders, pornography, child molestation, children rebelling, and being disrespectful, etc., and the list goes on. I like this scripture in 1 John 3:9 and 10.

Whosoever born of God doth not commit sin; for his seed remaineth in him: and he cannot sin, because he is born of God. (1 John 3:9)

Now check out verse 10.

In this the children of God are manifest, and the children of the devil: whosoever doeth not righteousness is not of God, neither he that loveth not his brother.

Let's check out some notes on these two verses to get more of an understanding! Here are some notes from my Bible. I have the Full Life Study Bible in the King James Version. Verse 3:9 means that one who is truly born of God cannot make sin as their way of life, because the life of God cannot exist in one who practices sin.

The new birth produces spiritual life resulting in an everlasting present relationship with God. Now a believer may occasionally lapse from God's high standard, but he will not continue in sin. Now here is what verse 10 says: John has warned the reader not to be deceived about the nature of salvation. Consequently, the believer must reject any theology or teaching which alleges that one can be out of fellowship with God and continue to sin and doing the works of the devil. Anyone who continues in sin is of the devil. Furthermore, what characterizes a true child of God is a love for God manifested in keeping His commandments and showing genuine concern for the spiritual and physical needs of other believers. So, tell me, what child of the devil would have love for God? That's right, none!

So go back to the beginning of this chapter. How is a baby or a child supposed to know what the meaning of your words are? You can preach to babies all you want to, but they will not understand what you are saying and therefore cannot make choices for themselves. Children are greatly influenced by their parents and by their peers.

Influence, now this word has been part of human nature from the very beginning. Influence could be for someone's good, or influence could be used for the wrong reason in order to stir one in the wrong direction and used for selfish reasoning. Influence is the highlight of one's life, whether good or bad. What is the definition of influence?

Influence: the power to change or affect someone or something; the power to cause changes without directly forcing them to happen; corrupt interference with authority for personal gain! Take a good look around you. Influence is everywhere. But unfortunately, evil influences are by far greater than the good. We live in a very sinful world because we are born into sin. Therefore, sin eats us alive; and if you are not a Christian, then you will not know what to do about the sin in your life and the evil influences that take over your thoughts and actions. The world has no love for the human race! And guess who rules the world? The devil! Now you know why people are committing crimes and killing each other. The world is so full of hate that it is being destroyed. But in this fallen chaotic world, hate is normal.

Evil diversions: Here is a scripture that is very important to a child of God.

Little children, let no man deceive you; he that doeth righteousness is righteous, even as he [God] is righteous. He that committeth sin is of the devil; for the devil sinneth from the beginning. For this purpose, the son of God was manifested, that he might destroy the works of the devil. (1 John 3:7–8)

Satan's way of life is to defy God, rebel against His love, and to break His laws. Satan's motive is to take the place of God and crush all who loves Him. Satan does his evil work through people who love his lies. There are plenty of power seekers, manipulators, and egotists who want to make a name for themselves. They also want to attract people to follow them. They will offer a new way, with the lure of a better life which matches what our sinful nature longs for. Their motive may appear to be worldly and humanly natural to them, and they probably do not even know that they are serving an evil master and contradicting the word of God.

So, is this how God designed us? No. God designed humans to be loved and to love the way that He loves us. And so, it is always painful to be hated or for our love to be rejected! Every time we look to the world to love us, we will be disappointed every time. The truth in love is sufficient to stir the world against us. But we are called from God to live and speak the truth, and without receiving God's love, you will be lost forever. So, whatever it may cost you, please keep on loving each other for Christ's sake.

Because Jesus Christ came to destroy the works of the devil, it should be unthinkable for Christians to live an unrighteous life or to encourage others to do so. One day, God's demolition of evil will be complete, when Satan and his agents will have no more liberty to lead people into rebellion. But until then, Christians have the responsibility to work with Christ and not against Him. Righteous living validates the gospel and demonstrates that the believers are following Christ. The desire and ability to live a righteous life only comes from the righteous one Jesus Christ Himself. Since this world is heavily influenced to do evil but only little of doing good, who will people listen to? Since God gave human knowledge of a free will, who do you think that people will listen to? You need to remember that the people whom you listen to will be the ones who shape your life! Listening is a choice based upon what you really want out of life. So, this means that the people of God should listen to Him because they desire to be with Him and His holiness. This is my desire. Is it yours? But why are so many people rejecting God and a desire to live for Him? The world has this feel-good agenda and for those who have a desire for the world's standards will listen to worldly wisdom. But those who have a desire for God will listen to Him.

I have asked people who do not serve God why they don't serve Him and why they do not go to church. Here is the answer I got. "I don't go to church because church is boring. And I don't serve God because God will ask me to stop doing the things that I like to do, like stop drinking, stop having sexual relationships or even one-night stands, stop hanging out at bars, stop smoking and doing drugs, stop watching bad movies with bad language, violence, etc., stop hanging out with bad influencing people who are doing these bad things, etc." These are just a few things to name, but I am sure you get the meaning. Before I became a Christian, I used to think all these things were fun, and at one time, I used to enjoy doing these things. But now I am a child of God, and I live my life to please God and not myself, for I know what my spiritual future holds in store for me. God says not to be conformed to this world.

Love not the world, neither the things that are in the world. If any man loves the world, the love of the father is not in him. For all that is in the world, the lust of the flesh, and the lust of the eyes, and the pride of life, is not of the father, bit is of the world. And the world passeth away, and the lust thereof: but he that doeth the will of God abideth forever. (1 John 2:15-17)

There are things that we must come to understand about this verse! We must realize that this present world system is evil and under the rules of Satan. This world system is corrupted. Therefore, we must despise and abhor what is evil and refuse to yield to various types of worldliness such as greed, envy, hate, selfishness, revenge, ungodly entertainment, immodesty, immorality, drugs, alcohol, etc. We must have our minds conformed to God's way of thinking and loving.

People of this world are absorbed with what they can do and get what they want in order to satisfy their desires. Their motivation is essential pro-self and anti=Christ and exactly replicates the motivation of Satan whom Jesus described as the person who likes to rule the world. Now on the

other hand, people who receive the word of God are not threatened by all that is evil. There is nothing the world can offer that will have an everlasting value. So, the listening test of who listens to whom is important to know for your future existence when you die and pass from this life to the next! Question: Where will you spend your eternity, or do you even know?

Believers find great comfort in knowing that God is greater and that He keeps His promises to those who believe and keeps His words. Now despite being surrounded by the evil ways of this world, we do not have to allow it to shape us into its mold. We all must live in this world, but you do not have to live by its ways, and you do not have to be like someone else to be who you are. God created you just the way He wanted you to be, and that's it.

4

The Cause of Empty Souls

Do you believe in empty souls? I do. People with an empty soul will often seek out some source of comfort from the things in this world to fulfill that empty void that is in their soul. People turn to drugs, alcohol, sex, deceit, lies, cheating, and they will even go to the length to kill if that is what it will take to fulfill their hungry soul. Due to the lack of knowledge, people do not know and understand that God is the lover of our soul and that only God can fulfill our desires and needs, not people. This is what God has to say about lacking the knowledge.

My people are destroyed for lack of knowledge; because thou hast rejected knowledge, I will also reject thee. (Hosea 4:6)

Woe unto them that lack knowledge. Here are six statements of judgment that causes destruction of the soul. This is the case for the hole in your soul: selfish greed, drunken conduct, mockery of God's power to judge their sins, distortion of God's moral standards, arrogance and pride, and perversion of justice.

So, what is the actual cause for someone to have an empty soul? Are we born with one or what? Though humans are born with a soul, I believe it is considered empty until they are fed. Parents need to feed the soul of their infant in order to live. But to what the parents who feeds their infant depends on the parents' beliefs. Now a parent can feed them the knowledge of God or knowledge of the world (Satan's way).

As a child grows with knowledge to learn right from wrong, then their soul begins to do the same. A child's soul grows as the body grows. And though our body will die, our soul never will. The soul will continue to live with what it was taught while living in the body on earth. This is the learning process. What the parent teaches the child will determine the child's destiny. A child's future is in the hands of their parents. There are two different ways a child can live as they become an adult. They can choose to live an evil life, or they can choose to live the good life.

So why do evil people live with an empty soul and the righteous people who live for God has their soul filled with happiness, love, joy, and peace? Those who live an evil and wicked, mean life will have a full soul too but of hate, greed, misery, etc. The devil likes to drain the love and peace out of your soul and fill it with his emptiness. The devil will literally suck the life out of you and your soul if you let him. The devil is the major reason and a very costly reason for people to have empty souls. So now here is my question to you. Is your soul empty or full? And if it is full, then what is it full of?

As the devil lurks around for empty souls, he finds many to devour. These devoured souls are the ones that need to be filled with the love of God. But as long as the devil can keep you convinced that you do not need God or that God does not care about you, then your soul will be reaching death's door with a price to pay. Your soul will pay the ultimate price once it leaves your body. Then of course, you know that the devil will be happy because that is his job, to destroy humans' souls! Unfortunately, the devil all too often gets his way. Look at how many souls he has claimed already. Don't let him claim your soul!

It is my desire to reach out to you in regards to filling your empty soul with the good news of Jesus Christ. For Jesus Christ, I am the one and the only one who can fulfill all of your needs and love you totally unconditionally. God loves you so much that He sent his only Son, Jesus Christ, to die for you. John 3:16 says, "For God so loved the world that he gave his only begotten son, that whoever believes in him should not parish but have everlasting life." It does not matter how bad you messed up. He loves you for who you are because He has created you, and believe me, because God cleaned me up, and now I live a happy life with a sense of belonging in God's loving kingdom. It's the best feeling of peace and comfort anyone could ask for. Just come to Him as you are. Here are a few scriptures that I really like.

Have mercy upon me God, according to your loving kindness according to the multitude of your tender mercies, blot out my transgressions. Wash me thoroughly from my iniquity, and cleanse me from my sin. (Psalm. 51:1-2)

Wash me, and I shall be whiter than snow. Make me hear joy and gladness. (Psalm .51:7-8)

Now as an adult, I have come to realize that at times I still suffer from some type of pain from my past. Yes, I serve my Lord every day, and Jesus Christ has cleansed me from all of my wicked and evil ways by His shed blood, and now I am made whole. When I looked into the mirror of my past, I did not like to see what I had become, so I changed it. Do you like what you see when you look in the mirror? If not, you too can change it. My friend, you can do the same, just cry out to God for help, for God is there in the midst of your pain waiting for you to call on Him. Now God will not remove your problems or erase your past, but He gives you the strength and the peace to live through them, and God will give you mighty courage and strength to overcome them. God will also use your trials as stepping stones to the next level in life. That, my friend, is how we grow! We must make mistakes to learn from them, but we do not have to face our mistakes alone. God is with us. Please just give God the chance to renew your life and to renew your spirit. You will never turn back to your old ways once you know how much God really loves you and really experience for yourself just how much God really does accept you just as you are. I know I will never turn back to my old ways. God saved me from my early grave, and I am so glad He did because if I would have died years ago, I would have gone to *hell* for sure because I did not know God, and I was not saved. But God has a divine purpose for me! That is why I am here today, to fulfill my God-given purpose before I reach my final destiny!

610 Destiny, let's talk about destiny. First of all, what does destiny mean? In *Roget's Super Thesaurus*, it means "fate, destination, future, serendipity, and something to be achieved." How does *fate* fit in our destiny? What does it have to do with one's final destiny? Here in the *Holman Illustrated Bible Dictionary*, it explains fate as something that must happen. The Old Testament speaks of death as the common fate of humankind. So here you see that all humans have their own destiny that calls us to something greater than ourselves. Destiny can also be considered as a goal, something that you have in mind that you want to accomplish before your final destiny. Here are a few scriptures.

Then Simeon blessed them and said to Mary his mother, behold this child is destines for the fall and rising of many. (Luke 2:34)

This child is Jesus Christ.

His life was already planned out from the beginning, and so is yours. God knew you before you were born.

Before I formed you in the womb, I knew you. (Jeremiah. 1:5)

My major goal in life is to reach the lost souls and those who are oppressed and to teach them that there is life beyond your grave and that life will not end at your final destiny of death! The choices we make today will affect our tomorrow, whether good or bad. And God declares in His word that we will reap what we sow. Have you heard the saying, "Whatever you sow you will also reap?" Well, that is not just some talk, just to be saying it. It is actually the truth! And yes, there is *life beyond your grave*! Check out what God says about reaping and sowing. "Do not be deceived, for God is not mocked; for whatever a man sows, that he will also reap" (Galatians 6:7). We must not deceive ourselves, because our actions do have consequences either for the good or for the bad. If we think otherwise, then we are only deceiving ourselves. "For he who sows to the flesh will of the flesh reap corruption, but he who sows to the spirit reap everlasting life" (Galatians 6:8). We must make peace with God and worship Him, for He is our only everlasting life. God promises us life with Him in eternity. This is so amazing and wonderful words of encouragement. My deepest desire is to spend eternity with God, so what is your deepest desire?

So, how does a person who does not know God deceive themselves? What if a person who does believe in God was to join a religious cult, how would they know that they are being deceived? The key word here is *believe*. It all depends on one's belief. Even religious cults believe in God. People even go as far as to say, "I know I'm going to heaven because I am a good person!" Oh, really! Let us see what God says about that!

John 3:3 says that, "Jesus answered and said to him, Most assuredly I say to you, Unless one is born again, he cannot see the kingdom of God."

Nicodemus said to him, "How can a man be born when he is old? Can he enter a second time into his mother's womb and be born?" Jesus answered, "Most assuredly, I say to you, Unless one is born of water and the spirit, he cannot enter the kingdom of God. That which is born of flesh is flesh, and that which is born of spirit is spirit.
(John 3:4–6)

See notes on this! *Holman Illustrated Bible Dictionary* says, "a special act of God in which the recipient is passive." God alone awakens the person spiritually through the power of His Holy Spirit. Both the Old Testament and the New Testament also speak of the renewing of the individual. So, now you have the answer to the question. But still, it is up to the belief of that individual. This is where people start to deceive themselves. If they do not understand what it really means to be born again, then they will lose out on the kingdom of God. Now let us find out what will happen to us when we deceive ourselves or let others deceive us. If we do not enter the kingdom of God, then where will we go? Obviously, to *hell*! Here is a scripture on the subject of hell.

Serpents, brood of vipers! how can you escape the condemnation of hell? (Matthew 23:33)

5

The Reality of Your Conscience

Reality cuts like a knife. It cuts to the deepest and sinful part of your soul. Who wants to face reality? Not many people want to, and certainly not many people do. Reality is very painful to face because it is the truth of everything that has been hidden in our heart. It is easier to deceive ourselves and believe in our own lies, thinking it to be the truth, than to face the hard-core facts of reality.

Every day people are cheating themselves out of the life that God has purposed for them. But why? Lies can hurt you more than the truth can! Although some would think that would be a lie too. What does *reality* and *conscience* have in common? First of all, I will give the understanding of both words.

Reality: the quality or state of being actual or true. The state or quality of being real; actual being or existence of anything; that which is not imagination; fiction or pretense! *Conscience*: the inner sense of what is right or wrong in one's conduct or motives, impelling one towards right action; the complex of ethical and moral principles that controls or inhibits the actions or thoughts of an individual.

So, if reality is something real or true, then how would that align with a conscience? Is our conscience something real? Although your conscience is real, it is different when faced with reality. Reality will not play tricks on you, but your conscience will. Your conscience can make whatever is real and make it seem like it is fake! And whatever is fake, make it seem real! But reality is real and cannot play tricks with your mind. Can a person trust their conscience and be safe to be guided by it? Can they trust reality? People seem to trust their conscience all the time, but reality is real whether they accept it and trust it or not.

Reality is something that cannot be taught, but our conscience can be taught either right or wrong. Reality cannot be taught how to lie or be manipulated. You cannot manipulate what is a fact! Reality becomes real to a human when they decide to accept what is true and allow their conscience into believing what is right. The human conscience can be distorted while reality remains real. Reality is the opposite of imagination, but one's imagination can be revealed through their conscience. So then, what does imagination mean?

Imagination: the faculty or action of producing ideas, especially, mental images of what is not present or has not been experienced, mental creative ability or the ability to deal resourcefully with unexpected or unusual problems and circumstances.

The human conscience can be manipulated, and the human conscience has a very powerful thought process that can be taught early on in childhood. Children have the wildest imaginations that can lead them into a world of a false sense of security. As an adult, they possess an evil conscience thinking that what is wrong is actually right. They have no concept of morals. Children learn what they are taught, and that is how the human conscience is formed. Yes, we are all born with a conscience, but we have no understanding of it until we are taught what it means.

Children are taught through actions whether it be parents, family, or friends. Children are followers of someone with a high influence on them, whether it would be right or wrong. It seems like a child's conscience starts with the imagination of what they see, hear, taste, or feel. Here is a question to ponder! Are babies born with a conscience? Here are a few scriptures.

Conscience, I say, not thine own, but of the other: for why is my liberty judged of another man's conscience. (1 Corinthians 10:29)

For then would they not have ceased to be offered? because that worshippers once purged should have had no more conscience of sins. (Hebrews 10:2)

Unto the pure all things are pure; but, unto them that are defiled and unbelieving is nothing pure; but even their mind and conscience is defiled. (Titus 1:15)

And herein do I exercise myself, to have always a conscience void of offense toward God, and toward men. (Acts 24:16)

But have renounced the hidden things of dishonesty, not walking in craftiness, nor handling the word of god deceitfully; but by manifestation of the truth commending ourselves to every man's conscience in the sight of God. (2 Corinthians 4:2)

So, here we have it that a blameless conscience is listed in scriptures as one of the essential weapons for a successful Christian life of one who is a very serious spiritual person. A good conscience involves an inner freedom of one's spirit that comes when we know that God is not offended by our thoughts and actions. When you allow your good conscience to be defiled, then your faith, your prayer life, your communion with God, and your life of good works will be seriously damaged. If one puts away their good conscience, then it will result in the weakness of their faith.

A conscience is a God-given capacity for human beings to exercise self-evaluation. Your conscience will always be a witness to something, whether it will be the truth or a lie. Your conscience will also tell you your actions if they are both apparent to God and other men's conscience. And your conscience is a servant of your value system. A weak or immature value system will produce a weak conscience, while a fully informed value system produces a strong sense of what is right or wrong.

Your conscience will verify the integrity of your heart. So, check your words and actions and see if they are in accordance with God's morals and values or are in accordance with the morals and values of the world.

Your conscience is a part of your soul that is most like God, and those who disbelieve God will have a difficult time explaining the existence of the human conscience. What about evolution? There is no way that evolution can account for this facet of the human spirit. The conscience of humans was awakened when Adam and Eve disobeyed God. When we choose to do evil, our conscience is violated, and emotional discomfort takes over in us. Whether we acknowledge God or not, we were created to have fellowship with our Creator, and when we do wrong, there comes upon us a sense that we are against our created purpose, and that feeling is deeply disturbing.

Every day people try to find many ways to clear their conscience, but history is repeated with examples of mankind's efforts to appease the conscience, and nothing works. So often people turn to other means of drowning out that inner voice that declares them guilty. Addictions, immorality, violence, and greed are often deeply rooted in the guilty conscience. So, then, people seek out their early death as a way of relieving their guilty conscience. But death is not the answer!

However, since only God can redeem a violated conscience, it is in the best interest of the guilt-ridden person to turn to God and ask for His forgiveness. Yes, that is right. We can have our conscience cleansed when we bring our sins, our failures, and our miserable attempts to appease God. For God says in Hebrews, "Let us draw near with a true heart in full assurance of faith, having our

hearts sprinkled from an evil conscience, and our bodies washed with pure water" (Hebrew 10:22). As a follower of Jesus Christ, we will always commit some form of sin in our life, but God is faithful and just to forgive. God provides a way for us to have our conscience cleared away. As God says in 1 John 1:9, "If we confess our sins, he is faithful and just to forgive us of our sins, and to cleanse us from all unrighteousness."

Note to those who are living with a guilty conscience.

For we must admit our guilt and sin to God and seek for His forgiveness and His cleansing for the removing of our guilt and the destruction of the power of sin in order to live in accordance to God and His will for our lives. Now you know that you can take this step in someone you have hurt and know that you will be forgiven. But, my dear friend, you really need to be sincere about it.

Now for those who have children or about to bring a child into this chaotic world, remember that children are born with a conscience, but it must be developed by what they are being taught. Also, God says in Proverbs 22:6, "Train up a child in the way he should go; and when he is old, he will not depart from it."

Christian training has, as its purpose, the dedication of our children to God and His will, accomplished by separating them from the evil influences of the world and instructing them in godly conduct. But some people may not be Christians but are considered to be good people with good morals and good intentions. So how would this affect a child's conscience? Though the child may learn right from wrong from the world's point of view, it still will not protect them from evil influences and having a corrupted conscience. It is only by God that a person can clear their conscience, and therefore, a child must learn God's ways. That is the difference between godly living and worldly living.

So, since babies are born with a conscience, they still have no knowledge of it. Evaluate yourself! How old were you when you could tell the difference between right and wrong and knew the concepts of your consequences? Did you fully understand the difference between good and evil? What was life like for you as a child growing up? And how did your childhood affect your adulthood? This next paragraph is about life behind bars as a teenager is being tried as an adult.

You hear about how a teenager, age thirteen, has committed such an awful crime, and the courts are trying to figure out how to judge this teenager. A thirteen-year-old that has committed such a vicious crime of killing someone, the courts decided to judge that teenager as an adult. Now what does that mean? The teenager's crime fits that of an adult's crime, something that an adult would do. But does the teenager fully understand their conscience of the crime they committed? Even adults, half the time, do not acknowledge their consequences of their crime! So how can you take a teenager's mind and judge it by an adult's mind? A teenager's brain is not fully developed. Yes, they should still be punished for the crime, but to what extent? How would God judge that teenager? So how old does a person have to be before God considers them to be held accountable for their sins? How old were you when life became real to you? When you started knowing a lie from the truth? How old were you when you started realizing what reality was and that you have a conscience? Remember, death has no age limit, but your consequences does!

Hell and destruction are never full; so the eyes of man are never satisfied. (Proverbs 27:20)

Hell from beneath is excited about you: to meet you at your coming; it stirs up the dead for you. (Isaiah 14:9)

They all shall speak and say to you: Have you also become weak as we? Have you become like us? (Isaiah 14:10)

Get commentaries for these scriptures.

You see, we all do have choices, and we can choose to make the right ones. But unfortunately, an individual's choice is based upon their beliefs. So, listen up, my friend! Life in itself can become so difficult, painful, and even confusing. But in all reality, life is what you make it with the knowledge and actions you put into it. You will get exactly out of life, what you exactly put into it. And there is absolutely no doubt about that. But you are never alone while making your choices! Just remember that God is always with you.

As God says in Psalm 23:4, "Yea, though I walk through the valley of the shadow of death, I will fear no evil; for you are with me; your rod and your staff, they comfort me." I love this scripture. I speak this scripture when I am afraid of something, because I know that no matter what I may be facing, God is with me. I know that God uses my trials for my good, because God uses my adversity as a bridge to have a deeper relationship with Him. I just got to praise God for that. God has never left me, and He never will. God even promises us that.

"Let your conduct be without covetousness; be content with such things as you have. For He Himself has said, 'I will never leave you, nor forsake you'" (Hebrew 13:5) This is so awesome to know. But how does one become content with such things? First of all, what does it mean to be content?

Content is comfort, delight, satisfaction, fulfillment, cheer, etc. So, in the fiery midst of our pain, how are we to be content, especially for someone who does not know Jesus Christ? God does exactly what He says He will do, whether we know Him or not. Why do you think Jesus Christ came to earth? He came to save the lost, mend the brokenhearted, and to give us comfort in times of our desperation. But God wants us to call out for Him! In this next chapter, I go into more detailed information about heaven and hell. We all will live in one of these two places beyond our grave. Life is so short and yet precious. Why do we continue in our sins and keep punishing Jesus Christ? Jesus Christ is always there for us, and He holds out His hand and says, "Take my hand, for I will lead you to everlasting life with thy Father which is in heaven." Too often, we, as mere humans, will tell Jesus no and that we can walk through this life on our own without any help from God. That is the first mistake people seem to take. We all want to be independent. But our independence will cause us to fail every time. And the worst thing is that our independence causes death, spiritually speaking.

How many times have you heard Jesus cry out for you? He wants to be the king in your life. Jesus wants to show you just how much He loves you, and if He had to die for you again, He would. How long will people keep choosing to reject Jesus and then ask where God is when they needed Him the most? Why do I feel so lost and nobody cares, or why is this happening to me? Have you ever thought about these questions yourself or thought that God was punishing you for something? What are people's reasoning for not believing in God or Jesus? Now here is something that puzzles me. I know a man who claims to be an atheist. He does not believe in God, but yet He does believe in Jesus. So, I asked Him why he believes in Jesus, but not God. His reply was, "Because Jesus once walked on this earth."

Then I asked him, "How do you know that?"

He then said, "Because that is what people and the churches said."

Then I asked him if he was there to see Jesus walk on earth.

He then said no.

I then asked him again, "Well, if you did not see Jesus with your own two eyes, then how do you know he once walked on earth?"

He then repeated, "That's because that is what people say."

I then said, "Well, people talk about God all the time and tell you things that He has done, and yet you don't believe in Him."

This gentleman also says that he prays. I asked him, "To Whom do you pray?" He said, "To me, I pray to myself!"

Then our conversation was over.

Now I have one more conversation I want you to read. This one is about a lady whose car caught fire. Now to begin with, this lady claims that she does not believe in God. Now as her car caught on fire, she would say, "Oh my god, my car."

Then I asked her, "Why are you saying 'oh my god' if you do not believe in God?" Then she said, "Well, you know, it is just a saying."

And I said, "No, God is actually real."

So back to the main point about the cause for empty souls! As people go about their day, they just walk around aimlessly. Yes, granted, people have jobs, places to go, and things to do. But is it more important than acknowledging their eternity? Do people even think about their eternity and where they will spend it when they die? How about you, do you think about your eternity? Believe me when I say that hell is a real place. Obviously, people know that heaven is real because they say that they will go to heaven when they die, even if they have done bad things. All humans do bad things, but God still loves me. This seems to be people's point of view for when they die. Now why is that? People do not seem to take life serious anymore. People may not realize this, but time is running out.

The end of the world as we know will end. I do not know when, but it will happen. If Jesus Christ was to come back right now, would you be ready to go with Him, or would you be left behind? Please think about this question! Are you prepared to face reality of the end-time? Remember, it is not too late to change your mind yet. As long as there is breath in your lungs, you have time to make things right with Jesus Christ. Please make your choice now while you have the chance! Thank you.

6

It's a Heart Matter

So, you may wonder, what does God actually mean when He speaks about the human heart and about it being corrupted? There is this scripture that talks about the way a person thinks his heart will be there too.

For as he thinketh in his heart, so is he. (Proverbs 23:7)

For where your treasure is, there will your heart be also.
(Matthew 6:21)

A good man out of the treasure of the heart bringeth forth good things; and an evil man out of the evil treasure bringeth forth evil things. (Matthew 12:35)

But those things which proceed out of the mouth come from the heart, and they defile the man. For out of the heart proceed evil thoughts, murders, adulteries, fornications, thefts, false witness and blasphemies! (Matthew.15:18–19)

The heart of men is defiled, which also means that they are separated from life, from salvation, and with any fellowship with Christ because of sins that come from the heart. So, what does the heart indicate? Is God talking about the physical heart, the muscle? Well, we cannot purify the physical heart and make it clean! So, when God speaks of the heart, He is indicating the inner part of human, the soul. When God speaks of the heart in His word, it is the totality of intellect, emotion, desire, and volition. All it takes is an impure heart to corrupt our thought process, our feelings, our words, and our actions. That is why we act upon what we think.

A person's heart is unclean and in need of serious cleansing. All humans are born with a sinful heart, and because we are born as sinners, it is natural to want to please ourselves instead of pleasing God. We must ask God to cleanse us from within, clearing our hearts and spirits for new thoughts and desires. Right conduct can only come from a clean heart and spirit. Our heart must be purified through Christ.

The heart that God speaks about is the spiritual part of us where our emotions and desires dwell, also known as "the inner man." The heart of all human beings has been affected since Adam and Eve. Here is another verse that will help identify the sin of human hearts.

The heart is deceitful above all things, and desperately wicked: who can know it? (Jeremiah 17:9)

Because of the fall of mankind, our mind, emotions, will, and our desires have been affected the deepest level of tainted sin. Humans have become too blind to just how pervasive the problem has become. We may not understand our own heart, but God does! God knows all of our secrets of our heart.

Shall God not search this out? for he knoweth the secrets of the heart. (Psalm 44:21)

Our biggest problem is not external but internal, and the result of our internal problem, every human has a heart problem. Your internal heart problem is more deadly than an external problem caused by a heart attack. A heart attack can only kill the body, but an internal heart problem can kill both the body and the soul. In order for someone to be saved both body and soul, they must have a change of heart! A change of heart that only God can give! Here you have a couple of scriptures of God creating a new heart in you.

For with the heart man believeth unto righteousness; and with the mouth confession is made unto salvation. (Romans-10:10)

In His grace, God can create a new and perfect heart within us. God promises us the He will revive the heart of the contrite ones.

A new heart also I will give you, and a new spirit I will put within you; and I will take away the stony heart of the flesh, and I will give you a heart of flesh. (Ezekiel 36:26)

God promises us to restore not only our physical heart but also our spiritual heart. This restoration involves giving us a new heart that is as tender as the flesh is, so that we will respond to God's word. God will also put His Holy Spirit within us. This work of God encompasses the new covenant established by Jesus Christ. The heart is the core of our being, and God speaks of high importance to keeping your heart pure. For the heart is the wellspring of your life.

Keep thy heart with all diligence; for out of it are the issues of life. (Proverbs 4:23)

Your heart is the wellspring of life for your desires and decisions that affect your life. Following God and knowing His ways involve a resolute decision to remain committed to Him and seeking first His kingdom and His righteousness. Failure to keep your heart with diligence will only result in a departure from the path of God's safety and the entrapment of a destructive behavior. It will keep you separated from God! This should not be the path that you would want to take, and if you are on this path right now, then get off it, for it is a very deadly path.

God's word gives us a broad biblical meaning of the word *heart*, for it is the hub of human personality that produces the things we would ordinarily describe as the mind. For example: Scriptures informs us that our grief, our desires, our understanding, thoughts, and reasoning, and most importantly, our faith and belief system are all the products of the heart. Now it is clearly said in God's word that the heart is a repository for good and evil and that what comes out of your mouth whether it be of good or of bad talk, it all begins in the heart. Read Luke 6:43–45:

For a good tree bringeth not forth corrupt fruit; neither doth a corrupt tree brings for good fruit. For every tree is known by his own fruit. For of thorns men do not gather figs, nor of a bramble bush gather they grapes. A good man out of the treasures of his heart bringeth forth that which is good; and an evil man out of the evil treasure of his heart bringeth forth that which is evil: for of the abundance of the heart his mouth speaketh.

The heart, the center of our being, determines our outward behavior, and deeds must be changed or converted. For no one can do God's will without the inward change of heart. So, have you had a change of heart yet? If not, then when will you have one?

Now consider this: It is so easy of how a hardened heart can dull one's ability to perceive and understand. Even a Christian can get a hardened heart. You may ask, how can a Christian harden their heart? It is very easy; it is called *fear*. When calamity arises in our lives, our hearts often fill up with fear, doubt, and concern. Now for a Christian, this is sad because it implies that our faith in God is very little and that they have very little faith in His promise to take care of us. That is just too sad.

So now you have here where sin plays the major role in all human hearts since the day you were born into sin. And sin that is not dealt with will only make the heart grow harder, then sin will desensitize the effect on the conscience and making it even more difficult to distinguish right from wrong. This is what God calls "a seared conscience."

Now the spirit speaketh expressly, that in the latter times some shall depart from the faith, giving heed to seducing spirits, and doctrines of devils. Speaking lies in hypocrisy; having their conscience seared with a hot iron. (1 Timothy 4:1–2)

Godless and wicked people who suppress the truth will eventually be given over to the sinful desires of their hardened hearts. I see this going on every day! Also, too many people will fall away from the faith because they fail to love the truth of God and resist their sinful trends. Humans are at war with themselves all the time. Their sinful desires want to fight against what is right in the eyes of God. We, as humans, it is natural for us to want to do things our own way and that we seem to think that we know what is best for ourselves. But in reality, we are only deceiving ourselves when we think like that. Humans seem to think that they know the right way.

Watch and pray, that ye enter not into temptation: the spirit indeed is willing, but the flesh is weak. (Matthew 26:41)

There is a way which seemeth right unto man, but the end thereof are the ways of death. (Proverbs 14:12)

Humanistic wisdom is such a poor basis for determining what is true or false and what is right or wrong. God's written revelation is the only infallible source for determining the right path of life. Our human ways have the seeds of death, and God's ways lead to eternal life. What about setbacks and disappointments or when we get discouraged? Well, that too has an effect on our heart. Although sin is the major cause, sin has such a wide variety of things that can damage the heart. Pride is also one of the leading factors. Pride can stop a person from loving and be loved. People think they are protecting their heart by building up pride to keep from getting hurt. Or pride will just make you think that you are better than others, when in reality, we are not. So, when it comes to having a setback or disappointments, not one of us are immune to trials here on earth. We all go through the valley of death. But with God on your side, you can walk through death's valley and rest assured that God is with you. Just as He promises us in His word, that He will not leave us or forsake us.

Let your conversation be without covetousness; and be content with such things as ye have: for he hath said, I will never leave thee, nor forsake thee. (Hebrews 13:5)

No matter how limited our possessions may be or how hard our circumstances may be, we never need to be afraid that God will leave us. So many times, I hear people ask, "Where is God when I needed Him the most?" Does this sound familiar to you? This next scripture is very good to ponder on when you are facing hardship.

The Lord is my helper, and I will not fear what man shall do unto me. (Hebrew 13:6)

As I close this chapter, I would like to ask you to do a serious heart check and see what is happening, for you never know when your physical heart will stop beating! Please do not wait until tomorrow or the next day, because it may not come. God never promised us that tomorrow will come. For today could be your last. So please do something about your heart check now while you still have

the time and air in your lungs. May the good Lord bless you as you're checking your heart!

7

The Hole in Your Soul

Oh, the pain in the dark souls of people, how it runs so deep! This hole has brought so much pain, and the more it is being fed, the more it hungers for more. There is no filling this empty soul that has a hole in it. How can this hole be patched up so it will no longer be empty? My soul cries out from the depths of darkness, and yet no one hears me. Is this how you feel? Does your soul have a hole in it? If so, please continue reading. For I have been in the depths of painful hell!

That lingering pain from this dark soul, oh, how it cries from the inside out. The fear of a guilt-ridden mind has become too painful to endure. Now as you plunge deeper and deeper into the darkness of this cold soul, the more horrifying it becomes. And the more horrifying it is, the more your soul is lost into the depths of hell. The enemy likes to feed your soul full of hatred, deceitfulness, revenge, idolatry, greed, adultery, selfishness, wickedness, and sexual immorality, but the worst of them all, to turn you away from loving God!

You see, the enemy, which is the devil, only comes to steal, kill, and to destroy what is God's. Satan will steal the most important thing you have! Life! Now the sad thing about life is that a lot of people do not acknowledge who they are living for or who they are serving. People seem to take life for granted. They seem to enjoy the pleasures of this world more than the pleasures of loving God! People are dying and going to hell every day because of their selfish choices. Living in darkness is much more exciting than living in the light of Christ. Now there are two types of darkness. There is the physical darkness which is called night time, and there is the spiritual darkness which means walking around with blinders on. People are blind to knowing God's truth. But their eyes are fully opened to the lies of this world. Stop and think about the physical darkness. When people do drugs, or go to a bar, or throw a party at their house, they mostly do it in the evening when it is getting dark or is dark. Yes, people do it all hours of the night and day, but mostly all hours of the night. Now why is that? Why do cockroaches come out when it is dark and then scatter when light is shown on them? For the same reason that humans do the same. They do not like the light! So why is the light so bothersome? Because in the light, secrets are revealed. Even God said that in His word.

Fear them not therefore, for there is nothing covered, that shall not be revealed, and hid, that shall not be known. (Matthew 10:26)

For there is no man that doeth anything in secret, and he himself seeketh to be known openly. If thou do these things, show thyself to the world. (John 7:4)

For it is a shame even to speak of those things which are done of them in secret. But all things that are reproved are made manifest by the light; for whosoever doth make manifest is light. (Ephesians 5:12– 13)

The vile sins of people who commit their sins in secret are so debased that it is so shameful to even speak of them or even to commit them. Man's unnatural form of sin which man has invented is so bad that even to describe them would be defilement to the mind of the listeners. Light reveals whatever is in the dark, and light also will bring a clear vision to what has been kept in the dark. This is basically the same with the spiritual background of all humans. Satan cannot stand the light of Christ, because Satan lives in darkness. Therefore, Satan destroys mankind by keeping them in the dark as Satan tries to hide all of his secrets by keeping humans in the dark. God reveals all of His secrets to humans so that we can live in the light of God's precious glory. That is Satan's biggest secret that he does not want humans to know. And if Satan can keep humans in the dark, then he is happy.

Satan wants to keep that hole in your soul empty for as long as he can, in hopes of keeping your soul until the day you die for good, physically and spiritually. That is his secret that he does not want anyone to know. Please do not let the devil deceive you and keep you in the dark. Do not let Satan take your life into his hands, for you will surely die. And I don't mean just the body will die; you will face the second death. Yes, there is such a thing as two deaths. Some will die twice while others will die only once. Christians who dedicate themselves to Christ and live for Him each and every day will only die once, and that is the physical death of the body. Those who do not live for God and continue living in the darkness with Satan will die both deaths. First, their body will die, and then come judgment day, they will die the second death, which is when their spirit that dies.

So, you see, sin reigns in everyone's life, and sin seems to be the enjoyment of everyone's entertainment. In the world today, it is like people would rather enjoy their sins and be happy while they are in them and would rather die being happy in their own sin than to live a life of holiness and righteousness for God! People say that God doesn't want us to have fun or that God does not care about them, yet they would rather go to hell than to live for God and do what is right. Go figure. People even go as far as thinking that God is like their parents. It's always no, no, no. Why can't we just live our life the way we want and enjoy what the world has to offer us? If children grow up in an abusive environment, then they think God is abusive too. I know this to be a fact, because I used to think that God was like my dad here on earth, cruel and mean, demanding us to live by His commands! That's how my dad was. But believe me, my friend, God is nowhere near like that. God is a fun and loving Father, and He only wants what is best for you! For God says in His word about our thoughts and our ways.

For my thoughts are not your thoughts, neither are your ways my ways, saith the Lord. For as the heavens are higher than the earth, so are my ways higher than yours, and my thoughts than your thoughts. (Isaiah 55:8–9)

Here is a little bit of understanding for these verses. God's thoughts and ways are not of a natural human! God does not have a mind like ours, for God's mind is pure and holy! And God certainly has no sin in His thoughts or ways! But humans can have a mind like God's, and their ways can follow His. Our hearts and minds can be renewed and transformed by seeking God and asking Him for His forgiveness. A human's greatest desire should be to live a life in conformity to the likeness of our Lord and that everything that we do will be pleasing to God. We can do this by abiding in His word and respond to His calling. You know that tug that you feel deep down in your heart.

We must seek for God with all of our heart while there is still time. God's time of salvation is limited, and tomorrow may never come. A day will come when God will no longer allow Himself to be found. Please do not wait until it is too late to ask God to help you live for Him. The power and effect of God's word are never cancelled or voided. God's word will bring such a beautiful spiritual life to those who receive Him or just condemnation, a life of living hell (spiritually speaking), to those who reject Him. Just remember that only God can fill the hole in your soul, and He promises that He will if only you allow Him to. So please allow Him to. This is the most important step in life that you will ever take, my friend. For God says, Seek ye the Lord while he may be found, call upon him while he is near. (Isaiah 55:6)

For he saith, I have heard thee in a time accepted, and in the day of salvation have I succoured thee: behold, now is thee accepted time; behold, now is the day of salvation. (2 Corinthians 6:2)

The whole key point of these two verses is that there will come a time when God will turn His back on those who keep choosing to reject Him. People always turn to God when it is convenient for them or when they are in need of God's help. But, my friend, this is not how life with God works. For our pathway of blessings is in seeking the Lord with all of your heart and turning away from your sins. God said that those who return to Him with a sincere heart will find Him and His mercy. People should not judge God by their own thoughts. God thinks and acts in ways that are beyond human imaginations.

Those who choose to seek the Lord and find Him will leave their past with great joy and will continue their journey with God's freedom from the curse of their sins. And they will enjoy the fruitfulness of God's grace and experience His mercy upon their soul. Life is so precious and valuable, so please do not take advantage of the gifts that God has given you.

8

Wounded Hearts, Broken Souls

In the first chapter, I mentioned about the actual cause for empty souls, but this chapter speaks about broken souls caused by a wounded heart! As you continue reading this book, please keep an open-mind. Thank you!

Because you may be wondering by now, *how does a wounded heart break your soul?* Good question! Have you ever had a wounded heart? A wound that runs so deep you are not able to kill the pain it is causing you? When nothing seems to take away the pain and you feel like your life is spinning out of control, you turn to drugs and alcohol to numb your pain, and even then, the pain is just too deep.

Well, that wound, if it does not get sewed up, it will rip your soul apart. People have wounded hearts for many reasons, but it takes God to sew those deep wounds. God sent His only begotten Son, Jesus Christ, to be tortured and die for every human's broken soul. Jesus Christ became wounded and broken so that we may be made whole and for us to live a life of having a heart like God's!

My friend, is your soul broken? What was the reasoning for your heart being wounded? Have you tried to mask your pain by medicating it? Believe me, nothing will ever work until you let God deal with your pain. Do not let the devil take your pain because all he will do is increase the intensity of it. Your soul will remain broken until you are ready to let God mend it. God has a very special way of touching lives that you do not need drugs or alcohol. Please do not take this out of context. I am not saying do not go to the doctor or have your doctor to give you pain medication, and I am not talking about physical pain that wounded your heart and broke your soul. I am talking about the emotional effect that runs deep into your soul. A human doctor cannot heal your wounded heart or sew your broken soul back together. I hope I clarified this more for you.

Love is a very precious feeling, and when that is taken from you, then the only thing you have left is hate. But hate, my friend, is not from God. It is from our worst enemy called the devil. You see, the devil likes to take away what God gives you, and the most precious thing is His love for all human kind. So, when a person's heart is wounded, it puts their soul in great jeopardy. It starts to drive that person insane, and when that happens, then that individual tries so hard to fill that empty hole in their soul because they are not able to fix the broken pieces. To cure this problem, many people fill their emptiness by tucking their heart away deep down inside of them and try to pretend they do not have one, for the fear of being wounded again. This is the mind's way of protecting the heart and their soul. But in time, they realize that there is no cure for a wounded heart and a broken soul. Some would rather not love at all than to love and lose what they have once loved!

Then evil likes to take over in them, and so then they become heartless individuals with not even a care in the world of what will happen, and their consequences that must be paid for. Take a very good look at yourself and ask, is this you? How is one supposed to seek out comfort for our soul? How can our hearts be healed if the individual does not know God? How do we know if God is there in the midst of our pain and suffering? People say that talking your problems out seems to help, but the person you are talking to cannot mend your soul or heal your wounded heart. You need to be careful about who you talk to. Now when talking does not take care of the problem, then that becomes a bigger problem, because then, people begin to take action to help solve their problems. The only action needed to be taken is the dropping to your knees and calling out for God to help you. God is always there for you and always ready to listen, and the best part is, God has all the answers.

Unfortunately, people seem to take the wrong actions with the wrong intent. People get revenge, because that is the human nature coming out. They act out on that old saying "an eye for an eye, and a tooth for a tooth." Though this is not the best choice to take without living with the consequences, this seems to be the only choice people like to take. They like to hurt those who have hurt them. It is their automatic defense mechanism, human nature as they call it.

Many people just flat-out do not care about their actions and their consequences. The pain is so deep that it turns their soul numb. Pain is usually the cause for people being driven to make bad choices. Even taking their own life into their own hands has been caused by some type of serious pain running too deep in their soul that they drown in it. It doesn't have to be this way! God has a plan for everyone's life, and He says that all you have to do is call out to Him, just look for Him. He is there with you! Before you decide to end everything and take a drastic turn in your life, I would like for you to read this verse and really think about it.

For whosoever findeth me findeth life, and shall obtain favour of the Lord. But he that sinneth against me wrongeth his own soul; all they that hate me love death. (Proverbs 8:35–36)

There is an assurance to all who seek out Christ, and they shall find what they are seeking for. What is that people are longing for and try so hard to find? Happiness, love, peace, and comfort! Well, God says you will not find any of this in the world. For it is only through Jesus Christ that can give us what we seek after! All who find Christ finds life in happiness, love, joy, and peace. Doom will be brought upon them who reject Jesus Christ. They destroy themselves because they have set themselves up for disappointment by thinking that they do not need Christ. They will surely die physically and spiritually. Those who offend Christ do the greatest wrong to themselves; they wrong their own soul, and therefore, they choose death. For this reason, this is why I believe that it is very crucial for people to get to know their maker before they take that last breath. God should be everyone's reason why they live, but people choose not to acknowledge that. What about you, what do you think? Do you believe that God is the reason for you living? And if God is not your reason, then what is? And why is that your reason? Everyone has a sense of awareness, and everyone wants to feel like they are a part of something greater than themselves! Just remember that without God in your life, you are already doomed for death. Our greatest lesson in life is to search for God in every area in your life, and when you have searched hard enough, you will find the answer to life's questions and for the reasoning for life's existence. Your life does have a purpose for living. In my next chapter, "A Soul's Hunger," I hope that you will find meaning for your life. Our soul hungers for righteousness.

9

An Empty Soul Is a Tormented Soul

The cause of a tormented soul is the emptiness of one's soul. How often do people study about their own soul? How often do you stop and think about your own? So, you may wonder how a person's soul can be empty, and what does it mean to be empty? First of all, you need to understand what a soul is and what the soul's purpose is for a human being. Here is some information about what a soul is and what its purpose is.

The soul of a human being is their conscience and their freedom of will. The soul will not die when the body dies. Yes, the human soul is awake and very much alive after your body dies and is buried. God has created all human beings in His image, but God does not have a soul. The soul is the physical existence of the human body. The soul is the innermost being of a person which is the greatest value in them. The human soul is immortal and cannot die. Though the soul is not the spirit, the physical body does have both. It can become very scary to think about your soul when you are dead in the body and knowing that death is not quiet; death is awake. Death is not the end, for death is the beginning of life.

Many people whose soul is being tormented don't even know that it is their soul that is in need of help. They live their life in some form of a fantasy world thinking that death is the answer to ending all of their problems and the pain that has been caused. When someone is empty, they tend to search for answers to what it is that they are looking for. They look for ways to fill that empty void, that hole in their soul, and if they are unable to succeed, then they choose to end their life, or they want to end their life. It is so sad how people will seek out worldly things to try and fill that empty void, when instead all they have to do is turn to God and ask Him to fill that emptiness with His mercy and love. If people who are lost and empty only knew more about the understanding of their soul and how their soul operates, then I believe there would be fewer suicides and more of saved souls going to heaven rather than going to hell.

The soul signifies the spiritual principle in a human. The human body shares in the dignity of "The Image of God," and it is a human body precisely because it is animated by a spiritual soul, and it is the whole human person that is intended to become, in the body of Christ, a temple of the spirit. Man, though made of body and soul, is a unity. All humans are obligated to regard their body as good and to hold it in honor since God has created it and will raise it up on the last day.

So why is it that people not often enough think about their soul's destiny and where they are going and in which direction their life is headed? Did you know that people usually spend most of their life searching for things that will make them stronger or to cure their struggles with bad habits, destructive behaviors, and addictions? It is the human desire to feel loved and accepted and to achieve more of a successful life, and we believe that it is in our self that fixes whatever it is that we achieve and to have the life that we always dreamed of. But to be honest with you, that is not true because we cannot fix ourselves no matter how hard we try to. For it is only God who knows a better way for you to live!

Have you ever found yourself trying to fix other people or even trying to fix yourself? And if you have, have you noticed that it did not work and you feel like a failure because of it? If you have answered yes, then you are right. We cannot fix a broken soul, not even our own soul—only God can. So, stop trying to fix what is not yours to fix! Way too often, people drive themselves crazy, and I mean literally crazy, all because they cannot fix what they feel needs to be fixed. Not often do you find people living with peace in their heart and mind when they are not able to fix what they think is broken and needs fixing. So, you have here the word *peace*. Why do people have a hard time finding peace in their time of needing to fix something or to fix someone? I believe because it is lack of control that they are not able to keep. People think that they need to be in control of everything, and when they lose that ability to take control, they become self-seeking to find a way to gain back their control and their need to fix the problem. Then it becomes a downward spiral from there, and things just get worse. Have you ever noticed that there is no true peace when you are in control? Now why is that? Because it is only God that has control, and only God has control of your destiny. For God knows what will happen before you know. When we try to take control of what God is controlling, we are only setting ourselves up for self-destruction!

Here is a prayer that works for me, and it will work for you if you truly believe and trust God for it to come to pass. Here it is!

God, please grant me the *serenity* to accept those things which I cannot change. God, please grant me the *courage* to accept only those things which I can change. God, please grant me the *wisdom* to know the difference.

So here are the three major key words to a healthy lifestyle. Without God in your life, it is impossible to live a life of peace! Now I will break down these three words and tell you what they mean and how you can apply them to your daily life. *Serenity*, what does serenity mean?

Serenity: the state of being calm, peaceful, and untroubled. The goal of peace is to reach a state of mind to being calm in the midst of your pain and adversity and for the need to be in control of situations.

Courage: the quality of the mind or spirit that enables a person to face difficulty, danger, pain, etc., without fear, bravery. Courage permits one to face extreme dangers and difficulties without fear, a form of boldness.

Wisdom: the quality of having experience, knowledge, and good judgment, the quality of being wise, common sense, or the ability to discern or judge what is true, and what is right. Without wisdom, there will be no serenity. There is no such thing as having any type of peace in the midst of doing any type of thing that is wrong to do. Basically, there is no peace in evildoings.

Now that you have insight on these three key words, let's look at how you can apply them to your life. Quote: This must be done on a daily basis, because it takes time to engrave something positive in your mind, especially during hard times when you are not able to control what it is that you think needs fixing.

First of all, you will not find this exact wording of this prayer in the Bible. But you will find serenity, courage, and wisdom in the Bible. All this prayer is just asking God to grant you these three key words and to help you apply them to your life. Here are some scriptures that will identify these three words.

Serenity/peace: how would this type of peace coming from God be described? This type of peace coming from God's word is wholeness. Peace is resting in God's sovereignty and the calming of internal conflict, and peace is the reconciliation with God.

Peace I leave with you, my peace I give unto you; not as the world giveth, give I unto you. Let not your heart be troubled, neither let it be afraid. (John 14:27)

Note: The type of peace that God is talking about is inward peace, an inward peace of the conscience that arises from a sense of pardoned sin and of reconciliation with God! What did Jesus mean when He said, "Not as the world gives?" The world gives its type of peace sparingly, selfishly, and only for a short period of time. The way the world gives peace is Satan's way of giving peace.

"Now, the Lord of peace himself give you peace always by all means" (2 Thessalonians 3:16). Note: Peace is not discontinuance from persecution, but it is the calming of the heart that can only come from faith in God.

Courage: how does God define His courage? God says that courageous people will risk their lives to do what is right. They will also risk their reputation to do what is right. Courage grows as we learn to trust in God more. "Be strong and of good courage, fear not, nor be afraid" (Deuteronomy. 1327 31:6). This scripture is about trusting God to lead you to your destiny and having the courage to do what God asks of you to do. "Wait on the good Lord: be of good courage and he shall strengthen thine heart" (Psalm. 27:14).

Wisdom: how can God's wisdom be applied to our life? Wisdom is the ability to apply knowledge to everyday life. Wisdom only comes by studying God's word and obeying what it says. God's wisdom is practical and must be applied to everyday life.

Be not wise in thine own eyes; fear the Lord and depart from evil. (Proverbs 3:7)

Happy is the man that findeth wisdom and the man that getteth understanding (Proverbs. 3:13)

The happy individual is the one who finds wisdom in knowing that Christ surpasses any profits that a man might get from money. Jesus Christ gives what money cannot buy.

Wisdom is the principle thig. Therefore, get wisdom, and with all thy getting, get understanding. (Proverbs. 4:7)

The first step in getting wisdom is motivation and determination. What we seek after in life is what we will receive. "For God giveth to a man that is good in his sight wisdom, and knowledge" (Ecclesiastes 2:26).

Note: God rewards righteousness and punishes sin. And to the one who pleases God, God will give his wisdom and knowledge.

"If any of you lack wisdom, let him ask of God that giveth to all men liberally, and upbraideth not; and it shall be given" (James. 1:5). We cannot face our problems in life with our own wisdom and expect good results. We all lack God's wisdom because we do not ask Him for His. We, as mere humans, who tend to want to solve our own problems with our own wisdom and understanding. But that is just it; we do not understand because we lack God's wisdom. God's wisdom means the spiritual capacity to see and evaluate life and conduct from God's point of view and not our own point of view. Humans are shallow-minded! We can receive wisdom by drawing near to God and in faith, asking for His wisdom to be bestowed upon us.

What does liberally and upbraideth mean?

Liberally: tending to give freely, generous, tolerant of the ideas, and the behavior of others!

Unbraideth: to find fault with, reproach, to charge with something wrong! Have you heard of the story about the little boy with his broken toy? Well, listen up, because this story is about true life and the reason for our problems becoming more challenging rather than easier. And this story also reminds me of why so many people are just too unhappy and miserable in today's society. It's a sad story but so true!

The story starts out with a little boy who has a broken toy, and he wants to fix it but lacks the knowledge to do it. So, the little boy went to his father and asked him if he would fix his toy. So, the father says, "Let me see your toy," but the little boy would not let go of the broken toy. And his father replied, "I cannot fix your toy if you do not let go of it." Wow, amazing. This is exactly how it is with God. We have a problem with brokenness, and we want to try and fix things ourselves, but when we run out of options and ideas, then God is saying, "Here, let me help you." We all want help and need help, but just like that little boy, we tend to hold on to what is broke. So here is my word of advice, my friend. Just let go of whatever it is that needs to be fixed and give it to God. The more you hang on and try to fix the problem yourself, then the more it becomes harder and gets all messed up. Then eventually it gets thrown away because it is beyond fixing. Just remember, God cannot fix what you are not willing to let go of. Sad, but so true!

My friend, is God asking you to give up something in your life that is broken? Is there someone in your life that you cannot fix and you wished they would change but can't? As long as we are the ones trying to fix ourselves or other people, we are only getting in the way of God. For God is the ultimate Creator and knows what needs to be done. Never underestimate God! May the good Lord bless you as you learn to let go!

10

A Soul's Hunger

People whose souls are in a constant state of hunger is usually caused by their soul being empty for righteousness too long. To the amazement of humans, we do not always seek out what is best for our soul while living on earth. We seem to think that life on this planet is the only life that we have; and therefore, we live the only way that has been taught to us since birth, whichever way that may be.

We often think more about our physical sense of the here and now. How often is it that people will think about their future of the afterlife? How about you? How often do you think about your life beyond your grave? Do you think about where you will spend eternity, or do you even know? Apparently, people do not think about their life beyond their grave. Either they do not believe or do not care, or maybe they do not know what is out there beyond death.

As I study the human life and watch people walking around aimlessly, yet they think they are going somewhere, it just amazes me how people can be so ignorant to the word of God, including me. I hear people talk about different things going on in their life and not once about what will go on in their afterlife. On other days, I see people with a sense of purpose. They have high-class fancy cars, fancy houses, and high-class paying jobs. Yes, granted they work hard for their money, but what are they aiming for in life, especially if they have achieved everything they wanted? They cannot take any of those things that they worked so hard for to their afterlife with them. While it is important to make a living and raise a family, this is not my purpose for this chapter. People forget the most valuable thing in their life is their eternity, their final destination. And to think of the saddest thing is they do not even teach their children about preparing themselves for their eternity. And this goes on for generation after generation. There are countless souls headed for hell, and many of them think it's a joke.

Only God knows the heart and the intentions of people, and God will be the judge of your heart. Think about your heart for a moment! Here is something to think about. Think of evil people who are behind bars for the crimes that they had committed, especially heinous crimes! Were they born evil just because they committed an evil crime? What good mother would ever think about their baby being born evil? So why are evil people committing these awful, evil crimes? Did their parents forget to teach them how to love as a child growing up? As for me, it really makes me think about how the world is and who is in control of it. We are not in control of this world, but people have their way of ruling it! People who have empty souls usually hunger for evil and wicked things of this earth and thinking that it is okay, when in reality, it's not. What excuse will people use when they are being questioned about God?

What is your soul hungry for? Is it hungry for the pleasures of this world or hungry for the pleasures of knowing God and His ways?

Blessed are they that do hunger and thirst after righteousness; for they shall be filled. (Matthew 5:6)

What do you think God is trying to tell you about this scripture? God makes it a promise for those who hunger and thirst for His righteousness. They are actually hungering and thirsty for God and His word. All people at one point in their life hunger and thirst for love, honesty, integrity, and justice in society; they look for holiness in churches; they look for a sense of belonging, a place to fit in. But what happens when none of this is fulfilled in someone's life? Evil and hate start to rot out their bones. People's hunger and thirst for God are being destroyed every day by the evil desires and the lust of this world. A thirsty soul for God is just as essential as water is for the body. When your soul stops being hungry and thirsty for God, you will die spiritually. Same as the body; without food and water, it will die physically. So be aware of the cares of this world and the pursuit of worldly things, because it will choke your hunger and thirst for God, and it will stop you from seeking after His righteousness. Now here is a really good scripture that fits in to the way the world thinks, Matthew 16:26. This scripture is basically about denying yourself while living in this world. Yes, you are living in the world, but you do not have to live by the world's standards. Like fame and money, you can have all you want of it, but what good does it do for you if you end up in hell because of it? Preparing yourself for eternity should be your top priority. Too many people sell themselves short and do not take their life seriously, and so because of those choices they make, they will pay the ultimate price for it. They will lose their life and their soul forever and eternally burn in hell. Think about your soul. Are you selling yourself short to try and gain the worldly things that cannot be taken with you when you die? God says that the redemption of your soul is precious. Do you think it is? God says it in His word, Psalm 49:8. God clearly stresses that both the futility of trusting in one's riches and the nature of all this earth has to offer, God declares that the person whose life consists in an abundance of worldly possessions or the worldly pleasures and fame rather than seeking after God and His kingdom will perish (death)! But for those who live for God, their soul will be redeemed from the grave. In other words, their soul will be rescued from the pit of hell. One of the greatest mysteries of life is how wicked and evil people can seem to enjoy the pleasures of material possessions and the prosperity that comes with it. Oh, the pleasure of having money, how fast it can destroy your soul. But the biggest problem people seem to trust so devotedly will be the ultimate thing that will fail them in the hour of their greatest need. Please do not let this be you! Your earthly pleasures cannot be enjoyed forever! And just think, it certainly will not prevent corruption from happening in their grave; and in the long run, it's the most devastating mistake any human in life can make, to trust in their wealth and fame and not trusting in God. To lose your soul in the end is not a fun way to die, and it is certainly not the best way to die. The best and most precious way to die is to die with Jesus Christ in your heart. Amen to that!

Now here is a way of thinking about the life of your soul's eternity. A person's redemption of life is very costly, and to exchange your soul for wealth and fame will only cost you. Jesus Christ paid a very high price for you. Christ gave His life so we can live. He paid the ultimate price that no human can ever pay for. And yet people still choose to live for the devil. What has the devil done for you lately? Was it anything worth dying for? The love of this world is a very contagious and a bad disease that is eating your soul alive and taking you to your grave earlier than expected. Such a wasted life, the grave now claims. As God says in His word,–nothing but the *blood of Jesus Christ* can cleanse you from your own diseased soul (Jeremiah. 33:8)! Our inward thoughts and motives should be the same as Jesus Christ's mind, and that is perfecting our holiness in the fear of God! We must learn to hate the sins that we commit, and we must learn to hate them on a daily basis, not just sometimes. So, you may think, how do I keep myself pure and cleansed? By allowing God to teach you, His ways! You may wonder, how does God talk to us, and how can I hear Him when He is talking to me? Well, here is my question to you. How do you know when the devil is talking to you? How do people every day listen to the devil and do the things that he tells you to do? Why do people have such an easy time listening and following the devil's advice and yet have the most difficult time listening to God and doing what He asks us to do? So, think about this question for a moment! Here is a scripture to help you think: 1 John 1:7. In 1 John, it indicates there are two ways of living. Either you are in the light of Christ or you are in the dark with the devil. Either you live God's ways or you live the devil's ways. There is no in-between. Those who continue to walk in the light will be continually cleansed from all of their sins. But if you walk in the dark, you have no knowledge of God and nothing in common with Him either. For there is no darkness in the light of God! Just think about it this way: In heaven, there is no shadows because there is no darkness. Here on earth you see your own shadow when you are in the sun, the light of day.

To walk in the light of Christ means to believe in the truth of God as it is revealed in His word and to make a sincere effort by His grace to follow it in word and in deed. Therefore, we must make a clean break of every form of ungodliness that would corrupt us. And therefore, we must keep on resisting the tempting desires that corrupt us more and more each given day. We must strive to live for God and His holy ways. For it is only God who can renew our soul through His precious Son, Jesus Christ. For without God, there is no other way to live a righteous life. Now I am going to step off this for a moment and ask you a serious question. "What is the love of your heart set on?" How will you choose what to set your heart on? For I truly hope and pray that you will choose to set your heart on the things of God and let Him guide you through this journey in life! Please do not take the easy way out of life, because it is only a cheap way, and that's why it's called the easy way out.

11

Life Has Its Purpose

This chapter reflects back to the first four chapters. Though these previous chapters talk about your soul, this chapter, "Life Has Its Purpose," relates to them a lot. Your soul has just as much as a purpose to live as your life in the body does! There is more to life than just living and dying; either you live with a purpose or live without a purpose. Unfortunately, many people die without knowing their purpose, or they die without fulfilling their purpose. Your purpose is a reality to life! No purpose can be known or fulfilled until you face the reality of your purpose. It is then that your understanding will be opened.

People often wonder what the purpose of life really is! They ask, "What is life about?" We live, we die, but for what purpose? Some people do not even have a clue, no matter how old they are! What is so sad is that people often found wandering around in life like they have no purpose and yet wonder what their purpose for living is. And the worst part is, too many people give up trying to search for their purpose, while others keep on searching and finding empty values, thinking their life has no value to it. But with all due respect, people need to turn their lives over to God and quit searching for meaningless answers. Only Jesus Christ is the answer.

God says in His word that He has a plan and a purpose for everyone in life. God does not leave anyone out. Love is the master key to life's purpose, but not as the way the world thinks what love is but the one and only way that God says what love is. God's love is unconditional, and God's love will conquer evil through any type of hardships there is! The world's way just does not love like that. The world's way of love is we only love those who love us back. God says that we are to love our enemy, but no one knows how to love their enemy, and even if they knew how, no one would. People think it is easier to hate their enemy than it is to love them. If our enemy hurts us, then we as mere humans want revenge. But God says that we are to *love* our enemies. Now just how easy is that when it totally goes against human will. For it is a human's natural instinct to get even when someone hurts us really bad. So how is it possible to love our enemies especially the way that God does? It's called "agape love," which is the highest form of love. Agape love can only be given through the grace of God, for God is love. I can honestly say that I have experienced agape love, and it's so amazing how I can love those who I used to hate or want to get revenge on. It's such a wonderful experience. All I had to do was ask God to show me how to love my enemies, and He did.

Now love comes with a high price to pay when you are in line with God's will. To love our enemies as God loves us, we must remember the purpose of Jesus Christ's death in remembering His tortured and bruised body on the cross. The only purpose in life that God has in mind is to love one another just as He does. But, of course, it will not be easy, because our human hearts are very prideful.

Now when God calls us to serve Him and to love just as He loves, we as humans war against our own souls because it does not seem natural to love our enemies the way that God does. Our souls are filled with hate, and the only thing the soul knows to do is to get revenge, and that is the sinful nature in all humans! With humans' natural instincts, it is just too impossible to love unconditionally. People just do not see the point in loving our enemies because loving our enemies is just too painful to do. What does loving our enemies do for us anyways, and what is its purpose? As a matter of fact, the word *unconditional* does not serve its purpose in the lives of those who do not care. What does unconditional mean? *Unconditional*: not limited by conditions.

People put price tags on other people's heads, or they give if only when given to them. We expect others to give to us what we think we deserve. But this is not how God operates. People even go as far as saying that it is too hard to live the way that God wants us to live! People would rather live their own life by their own rules, but then comes the results.

Too much death is happening in this world because of selfish and prideful hearts! Now that is what I call *wrongful death*. Yet love comes with a price to pay too. To love unconditionally the way that God loves us will call for some type of sacrifice. Jesus Christ ultimately sacrificed His life to love us. So, what are you willing to sacrifice to love your enemies just as God does? Now death may not be the answer for your sacrifice; it may be sickness instead, or it could cost you financially. No matter what the cost is, love will come with a price to pay. But believe me when I say that "it is truly worth it all." to love others as God loves us.

To know God and your purpose for your life, you first must acknowledge that you need God and to realize that you are sinful in His eyes and not our own eyes. Pain and suffering will bring you to a higher level at understanding God's way of loving, and yes, love does hurt. Now unfortunately, without knowing God, no one will ever know their true purpose for living.

Have you ever felt that sense of lost feeling with no hope for a better future for yourself? Have you ever become so caught up in a web of sin that it had literally drained you of any hope for a better future?

Though change may not come easy and will not happen just overnight, the life of your soul will still call for a price to pay in some kind of a way. But if you are willing to take that step of faith and decide that change is the best thing for you, then you must be willing to endure the ultimate price. Believe me, for I did. As I have become more willing to change, life has seemed to get a lot harder for me to endure, and, of course, it became more confusing too.

I knew what it was that I had to change, but at that time, I just did not know how to change it. When I soon had realized that change begins on the inside first, it was then and only then that I knew that only God could help me to change and what needed to be changed. For I knew that without God's help, I would be destined to fail every time! I did not like that thought, so I decided to change by asking God to help me and to show me where to start at.

I know that as I commit my ways to God, He will help me to change the things that I cannot change on my own, and God will prepare the way for me to face my future that I cannot predict for myself. I can totally trust God to be there for me and to prepare my future for me. God has promised me that He will bring everything to pass.

When someone has hit rock bottom and is at the lowest and the last moments of their lives, that is the best time to raise your head and look up, because God is looking down at you and holding out His hand to grab you. For when you start losing everything, that is when you will start gaining everything. The day you hit rock bottom will be the day you will learn how to start living again. Real life is found at the bottom of nowhere. You will find yourself in the middle of nowhere, for I have found myself there. For in the end, your weakest moments will become your strongest points in your life, for it is said that when you lose yourself, then that is when you will find yourself.

As the days of your life move on, you will notice that nothing will ever be the same and nothing will ever stay the same. Just remember that pain will bring change. Time in itself changes everything and there are only three major components in life that changes everything.

1.) Learn!
2.) Love!
3.) Live!

We *learn* to *love* as we *live*. For God, He is all love, and we learn to live through Him. And that, my friend, is what my life was at one time, and now I have a brand-new life ever since I met God and asked Him to take my life and my will, and do not ever allow me to take it back, because I do not want it back. Thank You, God!

When you start feeling pain that you can no longer endure, just remember you have God to turn to. He is there waiting to take your hand and comfort you. God loves you so much He will never leave you or forsake you, and last, He will never forget you. Your life is just too precious and too valuable for God to just leave you behind. So please just turn to God and ask Him for help. Believe me when I say *He will be there for you in the midst of your pain*. And that, my friend, is the purpose of life! At least for me, I believe it is.

12

Living Beyond Your Grave

Living beyond your grave!

Is there really such a thing? Does life even exist after we die? Well, here in this chapter, I will go on to explain what happens after we die a physical death and what our spirit does once it is separated from the physical body. Yes, our spirit does leave the body! And though the body is dead, the spirit is still alive.

All through the Bible, God speaks about heaven and hell, and which one we are to choose. One day as I was doing a Bible study, I came upon Luke 16:19–31, about the rich man and Lazarus. Now I have read this scripture and heard it preached many times before, but it never dawned on me fully of what it meant—until that day I did my study.

It was June 29, 2014. I was reading this book called *After Life* by Phil Sanders. For some odd reason, this is the only book that hit me like a rock. I have read other books about the afterlife, but this one just totally opened my eyes. And now that my eyes are opened, I will never be the same again. And my heart aches for the broken lost souls. My eyes are also wide open to my soul when I die. Yes, I do know where I am going, and I have nothing to fear. I will live in eternity with my good Lord Jesus who saved me from the pit of hell. Amen to that! So here is what I have to say!

Death! How often do people think about it, and what do they think about when they do think about death, especially if it is their own? For me, I often think about it a lot. And in return, I reflect back on each day that I live and the opportunities that God gives me. I can honestly say that I am blessed! But my heart aches for those who are not, for the lost souls who do not know the truth about their afterlife. I do believe that if people actually really knew and comprehended what will happen then chances are there would be less killings and especially less suicides. And suicide is the main topic for this book. For it is my aim to reach the ones who are in despair and think that life ends at death.

Think again.

As I continue in this chapter, I hope people can realize that a death by suicide cannot and will not enter into eternal peace with God. And this is the worst sin that can be committed, because there is no forgiveness of this sin, due to the fact you are no longer alive to ask God to forgive you. And you cannot ask God to forgive you before you decide to take your own life, because you know what you are doing and that you are not sorry for what you are about to do, and of course, you cannot repent from this sin. This is why it is so important to think before you act upon what you want to do. Because there is no returning back to life on earth and ask God for another chance.

So, I would like for you to take a moment and ask yourself, are you prepared to face life beyond your grave? Where do you think that you will go? Here are some scriptures to ponder on that will help you answer my question.

The rich man and Lazarus:

There was a certain rich man who was clothed in purple and fine7 linen and fared sumptuously every day. But there was a certain beggar named Lazarus, full of sores, who was laid at his gate, desiring to be fed with the crumbs which fell from the rich man's table. Moreover, the dogs came and licked his sores. So it was that the beggar died, and was carried by the angels to Abraham's bosom. The rich man also died and was buried. (Luke 16:19–22)

Bosom means chest, like you would do for a baby. You would take the baby to your chest to comfort the baby. Let's pause right here for a moment! Notice that when Lazarus died, he went to Abraham's bosom. But the rich man, where did he go? Let's see what God says as we continue reading.

And being in torment in Hades, he lifted up his eyes and saw Abraham afar off, and Lazarus in his bosom. (Luke 16:23)

The rich man went to Hades! But what is Hades? *Holman Illustrated Bible Dictionary* says in the New Testament, Hades can represent a place of torment for the wicked. So then, what does *bosom* mean? *Roget's Super Thesaurus* says, "breast, chest, bust, heart, emotions, soul, spirit, core, depths, inside." The lost soul's destiny is in a place of conscious torment. You are alive and awake after death.

Then he cried and said, "Father Abraham, have mercy on me, and send Lazarus that he may dip the tip of his finger in water and cool my tongue; for I am in torment in this flame." But Abraham said, "Son, remember that in your lifetime you received your good things, and likewise Lazarus evil things; but now he is comforted and you are tormented." (Luke 16:24–25)

Notice that both the rich man and Lazarus are both physically dead, but they are able to communicate beyond their graves, which, by the way, is called the spiritual realm.

"And besides all this, between us and you there is a great gulf fixed, so that those who want to pass from here to you cannot, nor can those from there pass to us." Then he said, "I beg you therefore, father, that you would send him to my father's house, for I have five brothers, that he may testify to them, lest they also come to this place of torment." Abraham said to him, "They have Moses and the prophets; let them hear them." And he said, "No, father Abraham; but if one goes to them from the dead, they will repent." (Luke 16:26–30)

Notice here he said "from the dead."

But he said to him, "If they do not hear Moses and the prophets, neither will they be persuaded though one rise from the dead." (Luke 16:31)

Isn't it so cool how people can talk to each other beyond their graves! But yet, it would also be very scary to think about our future beyond our graves. Well, it makes me wonder if how I live my life on earth will be the way I live my life after I am dead. Wow, this has shed a new light on the phrase *passed away*! Seriously, think about it! We *passed, away* into another realm of life! That, my friend, is so awesome to know! So, as you read and study on this subject, you should notice that our role on earth does change after death. The rich man on earth became poor in his afterlife, while Lazarus was poor on earth but became rich in his afterlife.

The moral to this story is that God tests the heart of man. Here are a few scriptures on tests: 1679

The refining pot is for silver and the furnace for gold, but the Lord tests the hearts. (Proverbs 17:3)

Oh, let the wickedness of the wicked come to an end, but establish the just; for the righteous God tests the hearts and minds. (Psalm 7:9)

So, what do you think God will see when He tests your heart? Just a good question to ponder on! Another thing to ponder on is Hades is not actually hell. So, you may wonder, what is Hades? Hades is actually just a resting place where the soul goes once it is departed from the body. For no one can enter neither heaven or hell until after judgment day! And yes, come judgment day, everyone will go to heaven to be judged, but not everyone will stay. Each individual has to be judged, and if your name is not found in the Lamb's Book of Life, then you will go to eternal punishment which is hell. Here are scriptures:

But there shall by no means enter it anything that defiles, or causes as abomination or a lie, but only those who are written in the Lambs' Book of Life. (Revelation 21:27)

And anyone not found written in the Book of Life was cast into the lake of fire. (Revelation 20:15)

Considering that God is totally pure and holy, there is certainly no way that sin, evil, wickedness, or any other type of defilement can enter His kingdom. Sin is what separated us from God to begin with. The ones whose names are written in the Lamb's Book of Life happens to be the ones who are saved, those who know Jesus Christ and accepted Him as their Lord and Savior and puts their trust in Him and repents from their sins. So now for the ones who think they don't need Christ and think they can control their own life, then they are doomed and deceived, and of course, they will be casted into the lake of fire after judgment day. God knew that there would be sin on this earth before He created Adam and Eve. So, this is why the lamb was slain. This lamb represents Jesus Christ. As it says in John 1:29, "The next day John saw Jesus coming toward him, and said, "Behold! The Lamb of God who takes away the sins of the world!'"

Jesus Christ, the Lamb of God, took the punishment that we deserved. Could you do that? Take the punishment of someone else's crime? A tortured, hard, brutal death for something that someone else has done? If not, then why can't you? Jesus Christ did it for us. If you say, "Well! I'm not Jesus," think again, because that will not justify your answer. For in God's word, God says that we are to do greater works than Jesus. "Most assuredly, I say to you, he who believes in Me, the works that I do he will do also; and greater works than these he will do, because I go to My Father" (John 14:12).

Now this sheds a new light on the way I read the parable about your faith and the mustard seed. The reason we can do greater works is because nothing is impossible to those who believe in God. But remember the key word here is *believe*. One must believe in God in order to exercise their faith. God works according to our faith in Him. And we must believe that God is all-powerful and can do all things.

As I was reading the notes in my Bible, I came across this saying. The work can be completed, because there are no immovable obstacles when you do things God's way and by His spirit only, not by our own. So, by now, I am sure you get an idea about how you are supposed to live your life, and that if you do not live it according to God's ways, then you know what will happen to you. Without God's Holy Spirit working in us, there is no way our human mind can comprehend the things of God! Our eyes can only see what we touch and cannot begin to fully understand what is true in God's heart and revealed what is in His word. The Bible would just in no way be comprehendible for our natural minds. So, take thought on this, my friend, and see for yourselves, and please just don't wait until it is too late. For you never know when your time to come to lay down in your casket is up. Be prepared now and turn away from your sins, please. God only wants one thing from you, *your heart*! Is that so much to ask for?

I know how hard it can be, because I was once in that position. Yes, it is hard to give up the sinful pleasures of life, and while they maybe pleasure now, they will be death to us in the end. So, do not let yourselves be deceived! In this next chapter, I will focus on "death by suicide." As I have mentioned it previously, I would like to take it a step further and focus more on an individual's reasoning for wanting to end their life. May the good Lord bless you as you continue reading this book!

13

Death's Valley of Hell

Think about the name of this chapter and ask yourself if life on earth can represent this chapter. At times I would think so! There are so many valleys that are full of death, but to think of them being in hell, why would I write about that? Hell longs for death every day and just waiting for the next soul to enter. Hell loves to swallow up death. Valleys are full of dead bodies. Just look at wars and how many people die in them, including children and babies. But what happens to the bodies when the war is over? They are thrown into a pit and dashed with gas or some type of inflammable liquid, and then they are burned. I wonder if anyone says a prayer for them before they get set on fire.

But why is fire a chosen method to get rid of all the bodies? You see, fire is used as a disinfectant for anything that will contaminate the earth. Well, could this be a reason why souls go to hell? God said nothing that is contaminated can be in His presence. If your soul is contaminated by your sins when you die, you cannot and will not enter the kingdom of God. Ephesians 5:5 and 6 talks about this. This verse deals with all individuals who are knowledgeable enough to understand the things of God. This verse does not pertain to babies and little children. Individuals who have a sense of knowledge who are immoral, impure, greedy, or just loving things of this world more than God are excluded from God's kingdom. People who commit such sins give clear evidence of one who is not saved—in other words, not a Christian.

The flames of hell are used for the same purpose. People's souls are being burned, and one day, when God makes the final judgment, all souls in hell will be wiped out, and God will go back to His original plan, a new heaven and a new earth! Here is the verse for this: "Heaven and earth shall pass away, but my words shall not pass away" (Matthew 24:35).

Hell is used for destroying the souls that were uncleansed, because these uncleansed souls cannot enter heaven! I often wonder what this world would be like if everyone thought about their afterlife and the afterlife of others. People have no fear for hell and certainly not for God. It's like as if life beyond the grave does not exist for many people. Many even go as far as thinking that life on earth is hell. They could never be more wrong. Think again, people! This chaotic world is no match to what hell is really like. Please do not wait till you die to find out! Just believe what God says about it. Just remember that *death* can knock on your door just as quick and easy as life can wake you up.

Hell is referred to as a place of eternal torment with fire reserved for the ungodly. The Bible teaches that a person's existence does not end at death of the physical body, but it will continue on. Hell is the terrifying reality of continuous punishment, the fire that shall never be quenched. There is wailing and the gnashing of teeth, and the grinding of your teeth in your sleep is no comparison to these gnashing teeth in that is in hell. But what people don't know is that there is a second death, and it is the soul of a human that will die. To clarify things, hell is not a place for death; it is a place of torment for your soul until judgement day. "And death and hell were cast into the lake of fire. This is the second death" (Revelation 20:14). The lake of fire! Stop and think on this for a moment. How will a human be affected by this? Well, I will break it down for you of what it is like, and you can decide from there of what you think about it! It speaks of tribulation, anguish, weeping and gnashing of teeth, everlasting destruction, a furnace of fire; it also speaks of chains of darkness, everlasting punishment, a fire that will never be put out, and there will be absolutely no rest for your soul day or night for eternity. This is exactly why it is a fearful thing to fall into the hands of a living God. Now back up. Remember I spoke about people not having any fear of hell and not even of God. Well, what I was indicating is that we are to fear God, because as God says in Matthew 10:28, the scripture you recently read, if people do not fear God, they will end up in hell, because without any fear of their consequences, they will just continue to live a corrupted life. So, what that scripture means is that we are to fear God in the way of acknowledging Him and the power He has to destroy or His power to save humans and their souls. I would rather fear God and keep His commands and know that I will be with Him than to live a life without fearing God and living worthlessly, then end up in hell because of my own selfish unfearful desires. The fear of the Lord will keep you on track. So please fear Him.

There are too many valleys full of dead bodies and too many of them in hell. The valley of hell is huge and is always sucking up death. So just a word of advice, be careful of how you live and who you are living for! People, please heed God's warnings and repent. Turn away from the evil desires in your heart, and let Christ cleanse you. All you have to do is just ask Him. Stop taking advantage of the life that God has given to you. Stop living your life for all of the wrong reasons. And please do not purchase that ticket to hell.

This world is so full of people that are in the business only for material gain in exchange for their spiritual cooperation. Don't let this be you! When you try and gain in life, what is it that you are trying to gain? A new house, a new car, a better-paying job, high-priced fancy clothes, and vacations? No matter what it is that you are trying to gain, the big question is, *is it worth losing your soul for*? People like to be set for life and even set for their children, but are they set for eternity?

14

The Valley of Decision

Please be advised when reading this chapter, there are contents that you may find intimating due to the crucial statements. But it is not my intention to place judgment or to criticize anyone. Please read this with an open and a nonjudgmental mindset.

Decisions, decisions, decisions—we all have them to make! God calls us all to choose. We must choose life or death. We cannot have the sinful pleasures of this world and serve God at the same time! You must live out your purpose on earth before you die.

Now as I have mentioned earlier in this book about death's valley of hell, I now want to talk about your choice of decisions before making that final choice to end your life. You see, there is always hope for you and your eternal soul. That hope is in Jesus Christ our Lord and Savior. You see, just in case you do not know Jesus Christ, He suffered a tortured death on the cross for everyone so that we all can live a sinless and redemptive life. God sent His only Son (Jesus Christ) to save us from death's valley of hell. And the good news is that if you believe in Jesus Christ and accept Him as your Lord and Savior, then you will automatically be reunited back to God, and your soul will be saved from the pit of hell. This must come from a sincere heart though. Read John 3:16. It was God who sent

His Son to die for us. That proves how much God loves us all. This verse is one of my favorites because it reveals God's heart and His purpose and how much His love embraces people. Just really stop and ponder on this scripture. Reflect on it and ask yourself, could you give up your only child and sentence your own child to death, just to save hard-core, cruel, and evil people from going to hell? Especially, child molesters, murders, some of the most hard-core monsters in prison, well, could you? Could you really give up your own child to save this fallen, chaotic, cruel, and evil world and do it with a love so strong that it would not matter who they are or what they have done wrong, and yet still be able to love and forgive them? Well, if you can't, that's okay, because God understands. That's why He did it. Even I do not believe that I could do such a thing. And I am very thankful to God that He does not ask me to do such a thing. I know it would be the hardest thing to do!

So, as you continue to make your decision, just drop to your knees and cry out for God to help you. God is never too far away to help you! As a matter of fact, God is just waiting for you to reach out to Him and ask for His hand full of love to comfort you. Believe me, God comforts me all the time, and my sins are never too bad for His forgiveness. So just let go and find out what God will do for you. You do not have to end your life just because of the torment of pain! I love God so much. 1836 He has always been there for me and always will be. He made a promise to everyone that He will never abandon us. Just read this peaceful scripture: "Let your conversation be without covetousness; and be content with such things as ye have: for he hath said, *I will never leave thee, nor forsake thee*" (Hebrews 13:5). I love this! It is so comforting to know that God will reveal Himself to every believer through His Holy Spirit. God's Holy Spirit makes known to us the personal presence of Jesus Christ in us. The believers have God's promises. So, what do you think now? Are you feeling any better, knowing you have someone to save you and knowing that you are not alone in this world or have to endure your pain on your own? God will give you the strength that you need to endure your pain and sufferings of this world. God did it for me and many of the people I know, and He will do it for you. This world has nothing to offer you, but God does! God knows your heart, and He certainly knows the pain that you are in. God does not take away your pain, but God will bear your pain with you. Just remember, pain brings change, and that is a good thing. Just look at Jesus Christ, His tortured body and horrific death on the cross. He went through pain that we will never comprehend, and yet His pain brought so much change for the better. He lived out His purpose on earth. Jesus Christ changed the world by the intense excruciating pain that He endured. And the best part is that Jesus Christ did it because He loves us! There is no better love than that! I just got to praise God for that. Thank You, Jesus!

So, have you considered talking to God and asking Him to help you? I hope so, because as for me, being a Christian, I love you too, and I want to help you. This is the reason for writing this book! Do you believe me now? God is here with you, right now! I would also like to inform you that God quenches the thirst and satisfies the hunger of those who seek Him and want to know Him more on a personal relationship. Yes, my friend, you can have a relationship with God. There is such a thing, though it is different from a physical relationship with someone you love because God is not a physical human being, and you cannot touch Him or hold Him. But God's love endures forever, and you can talk to Him, and He will speak to you through His word.

Too often, people try to soothe the ache that is in their soul by filling the emptiness left in their hearts. People try to fill that emptiness with what is only a temporary satisfaction that only God's presence can fill. So, let's not allow any false temptations and temporary satisfactions fill your emptiness. Just cry out to God, for He is Good all the time. Here is the scripture that tells you God will come through with what He promises.

For he satisfieth the longing soul, and filleth the hungry soul with goodness. (Psalm 107:9)

You see, this is what I love about God. God not only takes care of us human beings, but He also takes care of His creation. The birds of the air show us God's care for all of His creatures. You know if He feeds and waters His birds, then He feeds and waters the rest of His creatures, including all plant life. This scripture illustrates about how not to worry about the things in our life that causes us pain in any type of form. God takes care of us, no matter if we are good or bad people. But bad people will face the consequences of the wrong choices they made. Quote: This scripture is not intended about not working for a living. It is intended for us to live a worry-free life from our heavy burdens that weighs us down and causes us pain.

15

Predicting the Time of Your Death

Suicide! To predict your time of death, could it be done from our own human will? You hear about people committing suicide and dying at a premature age! But the question is, can a person actually predict their own time of death? Or does God not answer prayers? Here is where it all begins.

But first of all, I will break down the word *predict* to get a better understanding of timing. *Predict:* prophecy, forecast, envision, divine, etc.

1886 The definition of this word *predict* is very interesting because it determines your future. There are many fortune tellers, but are they real? Can they really predict what is going to happen? Well, I will leave that question up to you to decide. God is the only one in total control of our death, and only God can take our last breath from us. No matter how a person tries to die or a fortuneteller tells you certain things, only God has predestined your death before you were ever conceived in the womb.

God already knows the time of your death and how you will die!

According as he hath chosen us in him before the foundation of the world, that we would be holy and without blame before him in love. (Ephesians. 1:4)

God is the one who gave you breath, and He will be the one who takes it. God's timing is perfect and never delayed! Many times, there have been people all over the world who at one point or another in their life has tried to commit suicide, even tried to predict their own death, and yet they lived to tell the story, and of course, they are probably living with the consequences of trying to end their life. Some have permanent brain damage. But it just goes to show you that if it is not your time to go, nothing you do will make God take your life sooner than He wants to. And to top that off, people have even flatlined for hours and came back to life. So now who is in control of your life? Though it would make you stop and wonder how people would know. Back to the issue of suicide! Here is the definition of what suicide means and how people relate to it.

Suicide: self-destruction, self-murder, self-immolation, a permanent solution to a temporary problem.

Since suicide is a form of death, then why do some people live through their attempt and live to talk about it? Especially when the doctors say that they should have died, how can one live through such tragedy as this?

I heard of a woman who wanted to end her pain, so she shot herself in the chest, with the intentions of dying! She knew it was wrong to do it and even asked God to forgive her before she pulled the trigger. Guess what happened to her; she lived to tell she story. She felt her soul leave her body and go to hell. There she felt the pain and the severe torment that was more intense than what she felt while living on earth. But her soul did not stay there because God pulled her out of that pit of hell and returned her soul back to her body. She is now living again after her attempt with suicide. And so, you wonder, did she turn her life around and start living for God? Does she embrace her pain instead of trying to kill it? I have not heard from her since it happened. But I wonder the same thing about how she feels about life now!

When a person's heart stops beating, the doctors say you have about ten minutes to live. A person is not considered legally dead until after the brain stops functioning! Why do some live and some die? Is anyone more special than the other? Or does God play favoritism when it comes time for death to knock on your door? The answer is no; God does not have any favorites, for He is a fair and just God! Only God knows the intentions of our hearts and when the last time it will beat. When God gave life to human beings, it is a result of a special act of God in a different way from other living creatures that He created. A human's life stands in a different category from all other forms of life. Humans have this unique relationship of a divine life that puts God at the source of all human life. So, do we have complete control over our own destiny and predict our own time of death? I do not believe we do!

Here is something else for you to ponder on! What if you were able to predict your own time of death? or better yet, what if God allowed you to know the exact time, the exact date, and the exact way you are to die, what would you do? How would you prepare yourself for that appointed time? For me, that would be totally too scary for me to even think about. And I personally would not want to know. I am sure this would blow the idea of suicide out of the water. It would for me anyway. Here is a confession I will tell you about myself. I once asked God to tell me when I will die and how will I die. Now as I pondered upon my request, I started thinking to myself, *what if I did not like the way I am going to die? What if I died facing what I have always feared the most?* Then I was reminded to *be careful what you pray for*! I quickly asked God not to show me, for I do not want to know now. We all will die someday, and as for me, the best way to go is in my sleep. I do hope that will be the way that I die! It would be so much easier and less frightening. I would like for you to focus on the death of Jesus for a moment and really think about how He was severely tortured and then nailed to a cross. And most of all, think about the fact that Jesus knew He was going to die, and He knew how He was going to die. He even knew the reason for His death and what He must endure to accomplish God's will. Now if God told you that you would die being tortured and you had to endure your suffering and pain for a couple of days with no pain medicine and God told you why you must die, especially dying for the person who caused you the most pain, would you want to know the time and date and the reasoning for your death in advance? I wonder how many people would still try to commit suicide if God showed them the time, the way, and their reasoning for their death!

How about you? If you knew that your death would be painful and you had to be tortured for your death, would you still want to know in advance? Yes, there are people being tortured and killed every day, but did they know in advance that would happen to them? Let's say that God tells you in advance about your death, would you believe Him? Would you agree with God and prepare yourself for that predestined event? Or would you be scared? When people contemplate suicide, they are trying to find a way out to end their pain, and yet not acknowledge the agony Jesus Christ had to suffer and endure for us. God never promised life without pain.

There is not one human on earth that is exempt from pain. Granted, we all feel pain in many different ways for many different reasons. But I honestly believe that if people could experience the devastating, agonizing, tortured body of Jesus Christ and His blood that was shed on that cross, and if people could only imagine His brutal death, then maybe, just maybe, there would be less people taking their own lives! But people are too selfish and too into themselves; that is all they think about when contemplating suicide. But they will end up in hell just because of their own selfish motives. Like I said before, a permanent solution to a temporary problem! So sad!

16

Life's Most Horrifying Ending

This chapter has been carefully thought out as to how suicide is the most horrifying and painful death of all, no matter how quick or easy you take your life. As I continue praying and writing this chapter, I ask God to inspire me in doing so! This chapter is not written to mislead people but in hopes of helping those who are in despair thinking that death is the only answer to a life of heartaches.

This chapter includes the truth about what happens after one decides to take their own life instead of letting God do His will through you. People need to think about their consequences and the severe punishment they will face in their afterlife. This is no joke, people! Your life is not a game, and it should be taken seriously, especially your life beyond the grave.

As people tend to live their life in this chaotic, fallen world, they want to know how they can make their life work for them and their own immediate desires. They do not look for God's desires for themselves, no; instead, they look for their own desires to fill their heart. They look for fulfillment that never satisfies the soul. This is the society that we live in today, a society of drugs, alcohol, sexual immorality, violence, and greed that all too often destroys the soul. Just look at the graveyards full of dead bodies. People are just dying to get in. This is not meant as a joke either.

People glorify the use of alcohol, drugs, violence, and money, and of course, the use of their own bodies for sexual immorality and prostituting instead of glorifying God!

Suicide, whether it is purposely planned or accidently through drugs and alcohol, is usually not a very well-planned-out event as to where one's soul will be. Yes, a person can thoughtfully plan out their own death, but they forget about preparing for their consequences that will make an eternal judgment on their soul. How selfish and ignorant can one be not to plan for how they intend to face their own consequences! Yes, there is life beyond the grave. But make sure you know what lies beyond the grave before you make any final decisions, please. Many who contemplate their own death do not believe in the afterlife or just don't care about it. All they want is for their pain to go away, and in reality, the pain is only more intensifying. What a devastating choice to make. People need to be aware of their consequences. Here is a good question for you. If you knew exactly what the end results would be like and you knew that there would be hell to pay, would you still try to end your life? Do you think that other people if they knew ahead of time, would they be too scared to take their own life? Well, if not, I hope this book will help prepare you or someone before they decide that their life is all because of the tragic thought that life is not worth living for. Because believe me, your life is worth every second you breathe, for it is the breath that God gave to you. So don't waste it on foolish thinking! Always be prepared. Life is about being prepared every day because you never know when God will take your last breath. Death is upon everyone, and you will die, but please let it be God's decision and not your own.

As you continue to read this chapter, I ask you to focus on the end results of your life after death, where you will spend eternity! And please do not focus so much on your physical death, but focus on the eternal death if you did decide to take your life into your own hands. For God makes it very clear in His word that everyone is born with a spirit and a soul, and when the body dies, then the soul will separate from the body itself. And the spirit lives on in the spirit realm. So, you may wonder, is the soul and the spirit the same thing? The soul is of human being, and the spirit is of God.

Now there are three different spiritual realms. There is heaven, hell, and Hades. Hades is the place where all spirits go whether you are a Christian or a nonbeliever. No one will enter heaven or hell until after judgment day. But in Hades, there are two separate parts: one for the righteous who lived for God before they died and one for the wicked who turned away from God before they died.

And in between both places, there is this huge gap, and neither side can cross over to the other side. Read Luke 16:19–31. When God makes His final judgment and your name is written in the Lamb's Book of Life, you will spend eternity in heaven with God. But for those whose names are not written in the Lamb's Book of Life will be damned forever all eternity and will share part in the lake of fire. People may feel like this is not a fair punishment, but it is not about being fair, for life itself is not fair. It is about your soul living for Christ or living for the devil. Christ has promised us all the blessings He has for us when we choose to follow Him. Certainly, you cannot expect good things from the Lord if you are living a wicked and evil life. The devil is constantly on the go looking for empty souls to devour. Please don't let him devour your soul. As I move on to my next chapter called "Grieving over One's Death," you need to think about the ones who are left behind to mourn your death. Also, remember this: They will only grieve for a period of time, and then they will go on about their own life.

17

To Die Facing What You Fear the Most

If you were to die facing what you fear the most, what would it be, and why would it be that? As for me, to die with the courage to face my fears is better than to die being a coward and not to! As God says in Hebrews 10:31, "It is a fearful thing to fall into the hands of a living God!" and Hebrews 10:28, "Do not fear those who can kill the body but cannot kill the soul. But rather fear God who is able to destroy both soul and body in hell."

Fear! Such a unique subject that people often take for granted but totally do not understand it. People fear the strangest things, like flying in an airplane, crossing a street, swimming, driving a car, afraid of the dark, fear of heights, fear of thunder, fear of letting go, or going back to sleep after a bad dream. This is the type of fear we have no control over. But we have no fear over what we can control.

Question is, why? I believe people put their fear in the wrong perspective. (Example, heights). Some people are afraid of heights, or of the fear of falling and dying. But what part do they fear most? Could it be the pain they would feel? I don't think so because it's a quick death! Could it be the fear of dying? That I can imagine, because they have fear of the unknown consequences.

Swimming! Some people are afraid of water, for the fear of drowning. Why? I believe it is because it's the feeling of suffocation. Airplane! Some people are afraid of flying, for the fear of crashing. Why? Could it be they might feel pain if they lived or because they are afraid to die?

Afraid of going to sleep! Some people are afraid of going back to sleep, because whatever it was that made them scared, they fear it might actually happen. Afraid of the dark! Some people are afraid of the dark, for fear of the unknown. I can relate to this one because my brothers always teased me when I was a child about monsters under my bed. This has stuck with me through my adult years until I have chosen to follow Jesus. God's way of approaching fear is F—face, E—evidence, A— appearing, and R— recover. The devil's way of fear is F—false, E—evidence, A—appearing, R—real. So why are people afraid to let go? Because the fear of letting go is the fear that it will happen.

How would you explain these events why we are afraid? One key word sets it straight—death! For many people are afraid of dying! So then, why is it that so many people who want to end their own life are not afraid of death? But yet they fear other things!

I hear about suicide all the time, and it just agonizes my heart every time. For I know that I have no control over the world, and I just cannot reach out to everyone and mentor them! My heart just aches and cries out to God for the lost souls who do not understand their life's purpose. People are just totally clueless when it comes to the reality of their afterlife. Some even go as far as thinking that once you die, that is it. And some think that death is the only answer to ending all of their pain. But the worst thing that can happen is when someone commits suicide, they are leaving their guilt and shame upon their loved ones, but some may do it because of their loved ones. You know that old saying, "Well, I will show them. Watch this!" Do you know of anyone like this? Maybe it is you! Well, my friend, keep reading! For there is another way to live your life more effectively and abundantly. God even says so!

Death by suicide! Suicide seems to be the popular reason for someone's death. It is the easy way out. But people do not acknowledge that suicide is more than physical death; it is a spiritual death too and the worst presence your soul will be in. Just imagine how many people live their lives aimlessly and carelessly. These people have no hopes, goals, or dreams. They just wake up breathing and go on about their day without thinking past their narrow-mindedness. People are always in such a big hurry to get to nowhere. They think they are going somewhere when in reality they're not.

You see, there is no time in heaven like there is here on earth! God does not keep track of time, but He does keep track of us. So why do people live such foolish lives? The way the world looks, it looks like people only care about themselves. But do they? If they really think about themselves, then they would think about their life beyond their graves, or so you would think!

Some people are fortunate; they have near-death experiences or out-of-body experiences. And in return, these people have the chance to turn their life around and start living it for God. I believe that it is for an appointed time for these chosen people. "For the vision is yet for an appointed time; but at the end it will speak, and it will not lie" (Habakkuk 2:3).

God does not tell us everything that He knows. But He will let us know the things needed that we need to know in order for us to live out His commands and do His will. Animals do not fully understand humans, the same as we do not fully understand God. As it is written in Isaiah 55:8, "For my thoughts are not your thoughts, nor my ways your ways." It is us who must trust in Him to live out our life. So does death really remain a mystery, or is it to only the ones who do not know God? I often wonder myself! So many questions go unanswered because God will only let you know the things, He wants you to know. Let's just ponder on that thought for a minute. Just think, what if God told you everything that He knows, how would you respond? As for me, I am glad that I don't know everything that God knows, because I would not want to know when one of my loved ones was to die or how they would die! Another thing is, I certainly would not want to know who is going to hell or when a newborn baby will die. I would not want to know people's time on earth will expire. What about you, would you want to know? I believe that there is so much to God that our human minds cannot perceive. There is just no way a person can grasp all of what God knows!

18

Grieving over One's Death

Funerals! What is a funeral, and why do people celebrate them? First of all, you need to understand what funeral means.

Funeral: the ceremonies of honoring a dead person.

Really, honoring a dead person, why? They are dead, so why do people honor them? Does the dead person know what is going on, or is it for the satisfaction for ourselves? People believe that their loved one went home to be with their Lord. Yes, this is true for those who have accepted Christ as their Lord and Savior while they were alive on earth. But this is not true for the wicked and unsaved people.

So, as I get into this chapter, I would like for you to think about the loved ones who are left to grieve as they stand around your grave when you pass away. As the body is being lowered into the ground, those who are left living have no clue as to what is happening to the deceased spirit that has departed from their body. Have you ever wondered what people would say or what they would be doing while standing at your grave? What kind of memory do you want to leave behind for others to remember about you?

While the living has all these thoughts about the deceased going home to be with their Lord, the deceased is acknowledging the life they once lived.

Yes, as I have mentioned in a previous chapter, you do live beyond your grave. Now need I to remind you that both the living and the dead are conscious and awake. The living only acknowledges what is happening in human atmosphere while the deceased knows what is happening in the spiritual atmosphere. If only the living knew more about the afterlife and the truth to it all, then there would be more knees dropping to the ground and asking God for His forgiveness. People, please be advised—*hell is real.* Your soul will be tormented forever if you go there!

When people fail to heed God's warning signs, then they put their own life in jeopardy, and in return, they will reap what they sow and face eternal punishment when they pass away. Remember one thing: While your soul is in hell burning with no way of escape, your loved ones think that you are in a better place; they don't think about your soul being in hell. People really believe that their loved one is with God and enjoying the everlasting beautiful life. No one wants to think you went to hell and that your soul is burning forever, even though it is. Do not let your loved ones be deceived. This is why it is so important to live for God, not only for your own soul but also for the soul of others! I hear these words quite often when someone passes away: "They are in a better place now."

Oh, really, is hell a better place than living on earth? People just assume that the deceased is in a better place because they do not want to know the truth or even hear the truth. Example: if you know the deceased lived a wicked and evil life without serving God and you are the Christian and you know the truth, how would people respond to you if you told them the truth and said that their loved one who passed away is in hell? Even though you know the truth, how would they accept it, or would they accept it? What would they say to you? Well, God calls the Christian to speak the truth. This would not be an easy step to take at a grieving funeral. Think about this for a moment.

So, here is another question! Why do people use the term *passed away* when someone dies? The word *passed* literally means "to move past, completion, to go across or over an entrance, to cross, to go through a barrier, to undergo, to elapse or go through a period of time, to come to an end, to depart, to complete a course, to excrete from the body." The word *away* means "to or at a distance from a particular place, person, or thing, far apart, aside, in another direction, to another place," etc.

Those left living don't think about that person's final destiny. Do the dead think about their own final destiny? They think that death was their final destiny, at least until it happens to them. Now why is it that people do not think about the final destination of the dead? And why are we not prepared to face the afterlife? People need to be more aware of their afterlife so that they can be prepared to face their death knowing where they will be when they do pass.

When people grieve over their loved one who has passed away, they are not grieving because they are concerned for their loved one's spiritual life! They are grieving because the presence of their loved one is no longer with them. People are so wrapped up in losing the one they loved, and all they can think about is how they feel, not realizing the one who passed is the one who will endure the pain and suffering until the end, if they were not a Christian. It seems kind of selfish to me, but in the natural, it is normal behavior for people who do not know about the spirit realm of the afterlife and are not prepared for it. My friend, please prepare yourself before you pass away. It is my prayer that you do! Do not gamble with your life. While you are here on earth, you only have one shot at this and one life to live.

19

Rest in Peace (RIP)

So, what would be a reason why I would write a chapter as this one? Well, as I read RIP or hear the words *rest in peace* as someone stands over the grave of a deceased loved one, I often wonder why people say these words and what is going through their minds as they say them. Could it be that they think just because that loved one is dead that they are in peace and that they no longer have to feel the pain of life? It seems like that is what we, who are left living, want to think. But what we believe, is it the truth, or are we allowing ourselves to be deceived? Just think about this for a moment. What do you believe?

Here is a devastating fact. If you are not a Christian and you die, God makes it very clear that you will go to hell. Now back to the letters *R I-P*. I know of a few people who were not Christians when they passed away, and now they are being punished for their sins and the way they have lived. The living actually think that the deceased souls are resting in peace! This is what the living truly believes. Apparently, they were never warned of the consequences as to where one will go. The one who is deceased is now being burned and tormented day and night for eternity while their loved ones who are left living tells them to *rest in peace*. Too bad the dead cannot talk to the living and say that you will endure for all of eternity if you choose not to follow Jesus Christ and give your heart to God. Please surrender your heart and your whole life to God while there is still yet time!

There is no peace for the lost souls! Now if the living knew the truth about their loved one who died, you can sure bet that they would be very cautious about how they live their life and would be warning as many people as possible. My heart cries out to people who do not know the truth, because not only are they being deceived about their loved ones who passed away but that they are also being deceived for their own eternal soul. Think about what I am saying and ask God to help you, for time is very short. Time is but a breath between life and death!

As for me, it really bothers me to know that people do not know the truth about the afterlife of the deceased or even their own afterlife when they die. But all I can do is pray and trust God. God makes it so clear in His word about being prepared to face eternity each day we are given the chance to live. Are you prepared for eternity? Do you know what will happen when you die? But most of all, do you know the truth of what God says in His word? Well, this question all depends on if you are a Christian or not. You see, the Christian who dies knowing Christ and is a follower of Christ will have rest for their soul. Now for the ones who are not Christian and die without knowing Christ, will have no rest for their soul, and they definitely will never be in peace. Peace belongs to those who know Christ and not about how good of a person you were.

Yes, many people die being a good person and doing good things for people. But we are not the ones who can save ourselves from going to hell, but we can certainly put ourselves there. Christ is our redeemer, and only He can save us. There are plenty of scriptures in the Bible to back what I am saying, but for now, here is a scripture: "I will ransom them from the power of the grave; I will redeem them from death" (Hosea. 13:14).

God not only releases people from the power of death and the grave., He will also take away death's threat. God has the power to bring back people from certain extinction in a land of exile. He did it with Ezekiel with the dry bones (Ezekiel 4 through 10). God, once and for all, can remove the abiding menace of death on the basis of the victory won through the resurrection Jesus Christ. Note:

This pertains to people who are already saved before they die. Remember, if people die before having Jesus Christ as their Lord and Savior, God will not release them from the power of death or the grave. God saves people from death while they are alive and not after they are dead. This is why people cannot redeem themselves.

Jesus Christ paid the ultimate price to uphold God's word which is the driving force that holds all things together! The staggering cost of Jesus Christ's sacrifice substantiates the secure freedom into which we have been brought. Let's back up a little way to Luke! Luke 4:18 says, The spirit of the Lord is upon me, Because he has anointed me to preach the gospel to the poor; He has sent me to heal the brokenhearted, To proclaim liberty to the captives And recovery of sight to the blind, To set at liberty those who are oppressed.

But God will redeem my soul from the power of the grave, For He shall receive me. (Psalm. 49:15)

20

Remembering Life as It Was

Remembering life just as it was! Just a moment now, think about the last three words *as it was,* then the first word *remembering.* So, you may know by now what life will be like for you when you pass away and how life will be for others who are left grieving, thinking that your soul is in a better place, and on how God said that people will remember their past life on earth, their life as it was. So, question, how do you think that you will remember your life on earth as it was when you pass away? As for me, I want to remember myself as a good loving Christian who loved people as they were and a very forgiving person who forgave those who have hurt me. I want to remember my life on earth as having a meaning to serve God with all of my heart. And this is how I want people to remember me when I am gone, especially my husband, my children, my grandchildren, my great grandchildren, and my memories passed on to my next generation. But I know that the only way for this to happen is to live my life now, just the way as I would want it to be when I'm gone. We must leave a good impact on the world now while we are alive, because we will remember how we once lived it when we are dead.

Now think about the word *remembering.* You may think, yes, the Bible may be true, but how is a person supposed to remember anything if they are dead? One thing you should know, just because the brain is no longer active does not mean your conscience is. Your conscience is very much alive, and you will remember your life as it was on earth. Let's begin with the word *brain* and what is the major function of it.

Brain: though the human brain is an organ, it is the basis of our actions and thoughts, to become aware of something forgotten again, to bring back to one's *conscience.* The human brain is the most complex living structure in the universe and your memory.

What is a conscience, and how does it work in a person who is already dead? *Conscience:* the conscience is an aptitude, faculty, intuition, or judgment that assists in distinguishing right from wrong; moral judgment may derive from values or norms (principles and rules).

Now how does the conscience work when you are dead? The conscience is to be subordinated and informed by the revealed word of God. But the human conscience can be ruled by the devil too, and this happens when a person willfully acts against their conscience and continues sinning from the things they desire. This happens when they put away the guilt of their conscience! Once the human conscience is willfully ignored, then the conscience becomes seared, and the person no longer feels guilt or shame for their actions (1 Timothy 4:2).

Where is the memory stored at if the brain is dead? There are two parts: remembering and the mind.

Remembering: to be able to bring back a piece of information into your mind, to be kept in people's memories because of a particular action or quality, something remembered from the past, a recollection. To remember is a normal part of the activity of human mind. The *mind:* the element of a person that enables them to be aware of the world and their experiences, to think, and to feel, the faculty of consciousness and thought, a person's intellect. The mind is the activity of the brain where information is stored. The mind observes and monitors the flow of energy and information across time while modifying it by giving it characteristics and patterns. So, does the mind die when the body dies? Now here is one more word and its meaning! *Conscious:* having knowledge of something, aware of one's own existence, the thoughts and feelings, collectively, of an individual. Now what is the difference between conscience and conscious? *Conscience:* your conscience tells you the difference between right and wrong. It is a sense of quality of one's character and conduct, adherence to moral principles and consideration of fairness and justice. Conscience deals with your inner thoughts.

Conscious: your conscious tells you when you are aware of something, alert and awake. The human mind is compared to as a blank state and is theorized that all humans are born free of any knowledge of right from wrong or being aware of anything. As a baby grows, they start learning; they become conformed to whatever it is that they are being taught. As they grow into adulthood, they live out their experiences.

Now here is a thought to ponder on. Flashbacks! What are they, and is there such a thing after a person dies? Do we have flashbacks when we are dead in the body but awake in the spiritual realm? Are flashbacks a memory being relived? Well, let's see what the definition is! *Flashbacks:* they are involuntary memories, often reoccurring events, in which an individual has a sudden powerful reexperiencing of a past memory and sometimes so intense that the person relives the experience and is unable to fully recognize it as a memory and not something that is really happening.

So, since we will remember our life on earth after we pass away from this physical body, would we have flashbacks from our past life? Sure, gives you something to think about, doesn't it? Instead of just reading this book, then putting it down, I recommend you study and analyze what I am saying. All of these seem to play a big part in the brain, and they all intertwine with each other. But now what about babies and little children? They have a brain, a mind, and a conscience, but are they aware of what they have? Are they aware of who they are? And babies, do they remember anything, and if they did, would it be long-term or short-term memory? I will speak more on these subjects further on as you read. But for now, let's look at animals. They have a brain, and they have a memory, but what about a conscience and a conscious mind? What makes us different from animals? I do know that animals have no soul. They do not understand the concept of sin. So, because of that, does an animal sin? What kind of thoughts do they think? Is it like human thoughts? Animals do dream, and they do remember and know if they are being loved or abused. But animals do not go to heaven or hell when they die. God clearly states that when an animal dies, they return back to the ground because animals have no soul, and animals don't know what it means to live for God or the devil. But I have read some scriptures that speak of animals in heaven. (Isaiah 11:6).

God clearly reveals that humans are made in His image, but God never said that animals are made in His image! Since we are made in God's image, that means that we have a spirit, a soul, and a body. Read 1 Thessalonians 5:23. God formed Adam from the dust of the ground, which was his body, and then God breathed life into Adam's nostrils, which is the spirit of God, and then Adam became a living soul. As for animals, I'm not sure how God created them. But I am guessing God did the same for animal as He did Adam.

The soul is briefly defined as the nonmaterial aspects of the mind and emotions and will result from the union of the spirit and body. The soul, along with the spirit, will continue to live after an individual dies a physical death. Out of the three components of the human being (spirit, soul, and body), only the spirit and soul are indestructible and survive death to either live in heaven or live-in hell. God made humans to love and to worship Him, and animals were not created for that purpose.

Animals were actually created and put on earth for a means of food for humans to survive. Notice that if you were to kill an animal, you will not go to prison, but if you were to kill a human being, you would go to prison. When you go fishing, you kill fish to eat, and when you go hunting, you kill whatever it is that you are hunting for. And when an animal dies, it is not resurrected. But we as humans will be. And when God sent Jesus to die on the cross, God resurrected Jesus, and He does not resurrect animals. Jesus Christ did not die on the cross to save animals (1 Thessalonians 5:23).

Now back to remembering life as it was! Since we all will remember our lives here on earth after we are physically dead, how do you want to remember your life? The best thing anyone can do now, while they are alive, is to live their life to the fullest, just as God wants you to. How would you prefer to die? Do you want to die with love and peace in your heart, or do you want to die with evil and hate in your heart? You need to make that choice now before you die.

There is one more subject that I want to talk about, and that is about evil people charged with an awful crime, and they die before they get their time in the court. When an evil person who has killed someone or has molested a child, and they decide to take their life into their own hands to keep from facing prison, the public thinks that justice has not been served. But believe me, justice has been served because that person will answer to God, and that person faces eternal pain and suffering in hell for all of eternity. People need to realize that justice will be served one way or another. God will see to it that justice is served, and the wicked will not go unpunished or get away with anything. God is righteous in all that He does. People do not realize what life will be like for them beyond their grave. People, please just get right with God now while there is still yet time, and choose to live a life that is pleasing to God so that you will not have to go to hell for all of eternity. Don't worry about trying to clean up your life before you come to God, because God will clean you up. God loves you so much that there is just no way that any human being can fully grasp the concept of God's love. So just let go and let God. May the good Lord bless you as you continue on your journey of life! Now as I continue with this chapter, think about your life as you know it. What is it about life that makes it the most difficult challenge to conquer? Life itself is an everyday challenge that must be conquered. It seems like life has got you figured out, and life knows exactly what it wants to throw at you every day. The problem people have about life is trying to conquer the challenge of it with courage and a positive attitude. That there is the actual challenge! It takes courage to keep a positive attitude in this chaotic world today. I am not talking about just having a bad day; everyone has a bad day. What I am talking about is something that has a hold on your soul, and it takes courage to stay positive through conquering it. Here are some examples: People with addictions, people with terminal diseases like cancer, people with disabilities that will affect their ability to live a life of blessings, people who have been in accidents that cripples them, and the list just goes on and on, but I believe you get the idea of what I am talking about.

Many people live in a make-believe-world attitude because they do not want to face the reality of whatever it is that is challenging them, accepting life, as it is seems to scare people. Life seems to get in the way of your hopes, dreams, and goals, and therefore, it is easier to give up and walk away than to fight the challenge with courage and trying to stay positive is a serious challenge itself. So, remember that when life knocks you down, then that is the time to pick life up. Yes, life gets very heavy to pick up, but the more you try, the stronger you get.

I know how hard life can be because I live with my disability every day. I am blind, and I have to deal with challenging situations every day. It takes courage to be blind and still conquer life's challenges with a positive attitude. One of my greatest challenges is writing books. I wrote another book and published it. The name of my book is *The Courage to Be Blind* by Tate Publishing. Nothing is impossible with God on your side helping you! The most important thing about life that you need to remember is "how you are living it," because in the end, that is what you will be remembering. It is so sad to watch people as they fade away into darkness, and for those who choose not to endure life's challenging moments, they give up too easy instead of fighting the good fight of faith. The more we fight the challenges of life with faith, the more we learn to live a better life. The purpose of life is like having money. What good does it do us if we cannot work for it? Yes, we do need money to live and pay for things we need in life, but this is not my point. When you truly work hard for something, there is more value in it, and then you find the true meaning of life. Nothing you earn is easy to get. Happiness comes when you are truly seeking it!

21

Life's Unfolding Moment

As each day begins to unfold, you are never aware of what is about to happen! As I have mentioned in my previous chapter, "Remembering Life as It Was," many people live in a make-believe world because the pain is just too much to face reality. In order to be aware of what each day will bring, you need to be prepared for it! But the question is, how do you prepare for it? Your life is not yours to plan out. It is God who plans your life! People wake up each day being unprepared to face what life throws at them all because they make plans of how and what they are going to do for the day and yet not realizing that God likes to mess up your plans. What I mean is, if you want to make God laugh, tell Him your plans. Have you ever noticed those days when nothing seems to turn out right for you? Well, unfortunately, people who have *empty souls* will live their life aimlessly and dangerously.

When people who do not live for God, and watch as their life unfolds in front of them, they are often the ones who get confused to the understanding of why! Let's think about death for a moment. Women who have lost an unborn child in their pregnancy often wonder why and what was the purpose of it. Some even go as far as blaming God for their loss, but is God really at fault? Death has no time limit or age limit. Death happens to everyone. Death even happens to animals and other living things on earth.

For there is no life without death, and death has its perfect timing. Now what about a child born into this world with a birth defect? People often wonder why God would create such an awful thing, but is it really awful?

I know a friend that goes to church with me. She had a child that lived to be three years old. Within those three years, death was knocking on this child's door. As this child grew in age, she became very ill. At the age of three, she passed away. This was heartbreaking to the parents. But the story that my friend told me about being prepared to lose a loved one was just so "breathtaking!" Though no one can fully be prepared to face death, you can find the strength to let go and be at peace with death's decision. My friend was telling me about how painful it was for her to see her daughter having to suffer as much as she did and knowing there was not much the doctors could do for her daughter other than trying to make her comfortable while she was dying. The pain her child was in and the suffering her child had to endure was just too much for the mother to bear. My friend never blamed God because she knew there was a purpose for her child's death at such a young age. My friend also mentioned how God made her child perfect just the way she was, even though she was very sick. My friend is a Christian, and when her daughter passed away, my friend felt a sense of relief with peace in her heart, yet a sense of sadness for the loss that she will never see again while living on this earth. My friend was relieved that her daughter was no longer in pain and has to suffer. My friend also knew that her daughter went home to be with Jesus. As a Christian, we know these things to be the truth. But not all people are like my friend. I have another friend who is not a Christian, and she has lost her child at the age of three, and here is what my other friend says about losing her daughter. In 2012, I went to school for my blindness, and there I met a friend who was very angry all the time and very rude. She hated everything, and she just did not like to do anything but sleep. My friend told me that she was envious of me because I seemed to be happy all the time and that I am very active and like to walk to places a lot. I told her that I love to walk, and she said she hates it. She always wanted people to do things for her and got mad if we didn't. But anyway, I soon found out why she is the way she is. She told me how angry she was with God and why she was so angry with Him. Things started making sense to me. This is a sad story of what I am about to tell you about her daughter being hit by a car and dying.

My friend was telling me that one day, she was in her house with her mother while her daughter was outside playing in the yard with Grandpa. Now she said she heard the gate open but thought it was Grandpa. Then a few minutes later, they heard screeching tires and someone yelling. My friend went to go see what it was about, and someone said it was her daughter. As my friend got closer, she realized it was her daughter lying on the ground with tire marks across her stomach. Her daughter was crushed by the car. Now you can only imagine what she looked like. My friend said that she freaked out and started yelling at the driver. Now my friend said that her daughter's death was not the only thing that happened. Her husband blamed her for the death, and then they ended up in a nasty divorce. It is hard enough to lose your only child and get blamed for it, but to lose your husband too? my friend blamed God for everything that happened to her. And now my friend is blind, and she is still angry. As I listen to her story, I just cannot imagine the pain she is in and the resentment she has toward God, her husband, and the man that killed her daughter. I tried talking to her about God and why it happened, but it is very difficult to talk to someone whose heart has been shattered, and they blamed God for it. How do you tell someone in that situation that it is not God's fault and that God has a plan? To this very day, my friend cannot talk about it without blaming, and it has been about fifteen years since it all happened. Now she also mentioned that the driver was not drunk or on drugs, and he was not speeding. He just came around the corner when her daughter was picking up rocks in the street when he hit her. I still talk to her about God, and I have invited her to church. I am hoping that maybe someday she will forgive so she can move on and accept what has happened. She has been grieving all these years and has not lived a good life. She lives in fear and anger every day. I tell her that this is no way to live a life. But to her, it is the only way she wants to live.

So here I give two examples of two very different women, and neither one knows about each other. One is a Christian and serves God every day and accepts what life gives her, and the other one is not a Christian and cannot accept what life gives and still blames God for everything. So, what about you, how are you living your life? Are you playing the blame game too? We may never know the answer to our questions about why God does the things that He does, but I do know that it is for a divine purpose and that nothing on earth will last forever. God is always perfect in His timing and in His creation. God is also perfect when it comes to time for death. We may think that a person died at an early age or maybe even a premature death, but God said death came at a perfect time. We all know that life is full of sorrow and heartaches, but did you know that just to wake up breathing and living your life is one of life's precious blessings and that life itself is so full of God's blessings? People just need to acknowledge that each day they wake up. Take a good look at your life and the way it is going! How often do you look at your life as a blessing, and how often do you thank God for the bad things that happen to you? Or do you thank Him at all? People say that life is what you make it, so how often is that true in your own life? We do not make life work the way we want it to. How often does a drug addict say, "I want to make my life a living hell for myself. I take pleasure in making myself feel pain" I meant for this statement to be for someone who has not yet been a drug addict. Now they might say something like this when they become a drug addict, but certainly not before they become one. I would not believe so anyways.

When life becomes a burden for you to live, this is when you need to realize that something is about to unfold, and it may not be what you would like it to be. Are you ready to take on whatever it is that is about to unfold in your life? How is your attitude when it comes time for the bad things in life happen that happens to you? How do you deal with the bad things that happen, or do you deal with them at all? Problems do not go away by themselves! We either deal with them and face them head-on, or we ignore them and skip right into our make-believe world. As for me, I choose to face them head-on in prayer and ask God to help me to understand what lesson I am to learn from them. So, when bad things happen to you, please do not give up. Instead, persevere through them with courage and push life beyond its limits. Trust in God and lean not on your own understanding.

Acknowledge Him in all you do, and He will make your paths straight (Proverbs. 3:5–6). For it is then when life is really worth living! I've got to warn you though: You will encounter odds playing against you, but nothing is impossible for those who put their trust in God. Be prepared to beat the odds fighting against you! For life must be challenged to be worth of any value. Here are some scriptures that I like.

When we lean on our own understanding, it is very limited and is subject to error. Our understanding must, therefore, be enlightened by the word of God and led by the Holy Spirit. We must continuously pray for God's wisdom and for His will in our decisions and our everyday planning. In all of our plans and decisions, we should acknowledge God as our Lord and Savior and that His will should be our greatest desire. When we do this, God promises to direct our paths. He will lead us to His goals for us, and God will remove all obstacles, and He will enable us to make the right choices. But you must live by His ways and trust in Him.

Path! Let's focus on that word for a moment. What does path mean? And why do we follow a path?

Path: a way or a track laid down for walking, or made by continual treading, the route or course along which something travels or moves on it. Now life has only two paths in which people need to choose which one they will take. One path is wide and very easy to walk on an everyday basis, and the other one is long, narrow, and very difficult. Now the easy one leads to death, and the hard one leads to life. Unfortunately, people would rather die living the easy path than to live treading on the harder path. For it is easier to live in our comfort zone than to challenge ourselves beyond our limits. Just think of it this way: How many people would rather be a couch potato than to be an athlete?

So, the two paths are about our spiritual life. We can choose to live the devil's ways, which is easier and more enjoyable, or we can choose to live for God, which becomes more challenging. Life is more challenging living for God because we live in a fallen and sinful world where the devil is in control of it! Temptations are very challenging to overcome, but with God's help, it can be done. Not many people live for Jesus Christ or follow Him on that road that leads to life, for only a few will find it (Matthew 7:14).

Here is a more in-depth explanation. The gate is narrow, and the way is difficult. The way is the way of the Lord, and those who faithfully choose to follow Christ's teachings will find abundance in their life. They will have joy and peace even in bad times. You would wonder how in this world a person can have so much joy and peace in a time of despair. Well, this is how: follow the narrow path. Now here is the other path, which is the one people love to take, and it is the most popular one, but it is very destructive. This gate is the wide one and is very easy to live, or should I say "enjoyable".

This path is self-indulgence and pleasure which leads to self-destruction. The reason why the narrow gate is a difficult way to live is because when you live for Jesus Christ and choose to follow Him on a daily basis, it would require from your faith, discipline, and endurance. Think about that word, *discipline*. People do not like to be disciplined. And this all begins from the time we are born. Life is so much easier without all the rules, and this is why people choose the other gate. Can you honestly tell yourself and other people that you love to be disciplined? Only a Christian who is truly living for God will say that and mean it. I do. I love it when God disciplines me, for I know that He loves me. The same principle goes for your children. Yes, it does hurt, and at times, I do not like the consequences. When you truly love your Lord, you will want to keep His commands and teachings. God loves it when you are willing to obey His Son, and he is very near to those who have such willing and loving hearts. Now back to the question of how someone could be so happy and joyful and so full of peace when they are in a time of despair. Well, here is a scripture that will help you to understand: "Peace I leave with you, my peace I give unto you: not as the world giveth, give I unto you. Let not your heart be troubled, neither let it be afraid" (John 14:27).

This type of peace is an inward peace that only Christ can give, and no money in the world can buy it. This inward peace starts in the conscience that arises from the sense of sin that has been forgiven by Christ. It is not given as the world gives, which means selfishly, temporary, things that money can buy, sparingly; all this is a type of peace that cannot be fulfilled. So, when you have inward peace given by Christ, there is no need to be afraid and let your heart be troubled. Christ's peace gives you a sense of calmness in the middle of chaos. Now that is the peace I am talking about.

How does one get this type of peace, you may wonder? You must start with a sincere repentant (to turn away from your sin) heart and cry out in prayer, then you must let go and fully trust in God to bring it to pass. Then you may wonder, do I have to be a Christian? It would certainly help. People who are not Christians do not understand the works of Christ, so they choose not to obey. A true and dedicated Christian will not follow the ways of this world because they know the world has nothing to offer them that will last. God is real, and so are His promises. Amen to that.

This next chapter is based on choosing the wrong path.

22

Tormented by Fear

A tormented soul can be caused by many different reasons and a variety of self-destructive behaviors. There is one in particular that I will focus on, and that is *fear*! Now it seems to me that will take the people's behavior to an extreme level that is beyond comprehension. Fear will torment and haunt you for life, that is, if we choose to let it! When you allow fear to torment your soul, it will haunt you until something drastic happens to you. Your soul then is left to bear the pain caused by your own beliefs of whatever it is that is causing you to fear. Your beliefs play a major role in your life! You can choose to be what it is that you fear will happen, or you can choose to stop letting fear dominate your thoughts. Yes, I know it is easier said than done. I have been there and done that! But it's true that what you believe will determine how your soul will be affected!

Have you ever felt that agonizing, gut-wrenching feeling that literally made you feel sick to your stomach? Have you ever wondered what it is that is making you feel afraid? And have you ever identified what it was that has caused you such painful torment? What about being locked inside of your own fear of something that has never happened? Well, I have! But please take some thought on this, because sometimes if you think on your fear too much, it can happen. This has happened to me! There are so many things in life that I have been afraid of, and many times that fear has tormented me to the point that I felt like I was losing my mind. There have also been many things that I could not identify what it was that I feared. But for now, I will only give a few examples of some of the things I feared most.

February 19, 2012, I started school for my blindness at the Department for the Blind in Seattle, Washington. I was born with retinitis pigmentosa, and the doctors say that there is no cure for this eye disease. Well, as school goes, when I first started, I thought to myself, *this school is not for me!* I said to myself that I am not blind; I just have a vision problem, and social security calls it legally blind. I am partially blind, not blind. I thought that there was a difference between being blind and only being partially blind. That is until I joined their seminars. The school had a seminar once a week. The seminars all dealt over each student talking about their blindness, their fears, and why they decided to come to school. The first couple of seminars I just could not face reality. I still thought that this school was not for me. I did not want to face reality, and I certainly was not prepared to that is, until March of 2012. And then that was a doozy for me. Now this may seem a bit odd, but I do not remember the exact date that this one special seminar was and that it would be my future blessing. Now I was not prepared to accept what was about to happen to me.

Reality, yes, reality! Reality hit me like a rock, and I did not like it one bit. But for future reference, reality has set me free, and I am so glad I went to school! Well, this was when I finally realized what reality meant and that I had to face it. Ouch, not good! Accepting my eye blindness hit me really hard! I did not want to accept it. All my life I have lived in fear, and I did not even realize that until I went to school for my blindness. But to be honest with myself, I knew I had to face reality because I could not change what was happening to me. By hanging onto denial and fearing to accept it only tormented me more. I was afraid to accept my blindness and move on because I thought people would think of me in a different way or make in front of me. I was afraid of losing my independence. So, if I walked around acting like I'm not blind, then I felt adequate. But if I had to walk around with a cane representing my blindness, then I really felt inadequate. But in all reality, I was actually being tormented and really selfish to think that my blindness can be used for a greater purpose in life.

I would fall more, run into things more, or bump into people. Without my cane, I ended up in the hospital more. And then people would get mad at me and say, "What is wrong with you? Are you blind or something?" This really would hurt me, to know how people treat you. But they didn't know that I was blind, so they were entitled to think what they wanted to think. But now that I walk with my cane, people are aware of my blindness, and they are more courteous and helpful with me.

People even watch out for me more! The worst fear I had was that I would never see the faces of my grandchildren again, and to me, that would be the most devastating thing to have to face in life, or so I thought until I took a plane to Pennsylvania. Now I have always been afraid of flying in a plane, big or small. This is my second greatest fear! So before going on to my second greatest fear, I will take you back to my teenage years when I first flew on an airplane. This was when my second fear took place and has escalated from there.

When I was thirteen, I was living in Wyoming, and my mother sent me to visit my father who had lived in Washington. My father was really good friends with a man who had owned a private four passenger airplane. So, when my visit was over, my father had sent me and my brother back to Wyoming on his friend's airplane. I did not know I was afraid of airplanes until I was on it. That airplane looked like it was going to hit the trees; it really seemed that close. But the pilot assured me that the plane was higher up than what it seemed. And yes, he was right. But it sure did not seem like it. Then the plane hit many air pockets and made the plane feel like it was out of control, and I thought we were going to crash. Again, the pilot reminded me that everything was okay, and it was. Though everything was okay, I was given air sickness medicine that made me sleep through the rest of the trip. As I woke up, I was still feeling sick, so the pilot opened the air vent, and the air was cold but felt good. My brother seemed to have enjoyed the trip, and he was certainly not afraid. So as for me, I will never forget that feeling of fear that was in the pit of my stomach. From then on, I have always been afraid of planes until I flew to Pennsylvania to visit my daughter. Now here is where I will tell you about my second greatest fear.

On September 9, 2014, I took a plane to Pennsylvania. Now just days before my trip to Pennsylvania, I kept feeling a tormented type of feeling like I had when I was thirteen. And then a few days later, I had a bad dream that the plane I was on had crashed into the water. It was a river, but I didn't know where. Now when the plane had plunged into the water, I started praying and saying God will save us—I know He will! Then the plane came partway up out of the water and plunged again. This happened a few times, and then the last time that the plane had plunged back into the water, it had merged under a bridge, and the plane could not surface. I then started trying to kick out a window, and I realized that I may not make it out of this plane alive. And I am not sure what happened after that because the dream had ended. This dream did not make things better for me; it made my fear grow more intense. Wow, what a way to start off a new trip, especially clear across the United States.

So, as my life continues on this journey of mine, I have learned to never fear your past mistakes or be ashamed of them, because they are the reason you can move on and enjoy life, if you channel them right and learn to endure your mistakes or even the mistakes that others made upon you. I know it sounds easier said than it is done, especially for those who have lived a very traumatic childhood life. But God asks you to turn your rocks into stepping stones and then watch what God will do for you and for your future. God is not deaf, and He still answers prayers.

I know from my own experience that childhood traumatic memories can be horrifying. I lived a traumatic childhood life of abuse and on into my adulthood life. But it was not until I got older and turned my life over to God that I had realized that God is nowhere close to the image I had of Him. I had placed an image of God as being like my earthly father was. My father is gone now, bless his heart. He passed away. I miss my father, but I do not miss the traumatizing events that took place7 when I was a child. But God says in His word that His ways and His thoughts are nothing like ours (Isaiah 55:8). God's thoughts are not of the earthly, human realm! His thoughts are of the spirit, for God is not a human being. God is our creator who knew all human beings before we were created in our mother's womb. Just remember that when God's plans start to unfold day by day and God reveals His plans to us, it is then that we must remember that there is nothing to fear. Here is one of my favorite scriptures when I am faced with fear and not knowing what God has planned for me: "Be not afraid of sudden fear, neither of the desolation of the wicked when it cometh" (Proverbs 3:25).

This scripture speaks of God knowing who you are and what plans God has for you before He even formed you. Now in the book of Jeremiah, God had ordained Jeremiah to be a prophet for the nations before Jeremiah was even formed in his mother's womb. So just think about this verse for a moment! What kind of plan do you think God has for you? And when you ponder on this verse, you can actually realize that all humans were spiritual beings before we became human beings. Now here is what I call a blessing to have, that the human mind and heart can be renewed and transformed in the image of God by seeking for Him and His ways and wanting to live a better life. So here is my question to you that would help you identify yourself and what plans God has for you. What makes people so different from angels? Angels do not have a physical body! Angels do not die—we do! So, why did God create humans different from His angels? I believe it is because God has a goal for humans to live accordingly to His will and to allow Him to fulfill His plan in us. But living according to God's plan involves pain and suffering, and nevertheless, God's plans will always work for our good. Just really think hard about this next scripture. As for me, I feel the love and joy each time I am faced with a challenge and struggle to endure the pain from it.

And we know that all things work together for good to them that love God, to them who are called according to his purpose. (Romans 8:28)

This scripture greatly encourages us that God will certainly bring the good out of anything that is bad or that is meant to do us harm. Our pain and suffering will be turned into joy and happiness. During this transformation, God will conform us to the image of His Son, Jesus Christ. This verse also should not be taken out of context. This verse is specifically for Christians who choose to live according to God's ways. God will not turn our intentionally sinful ways and negligent ways to the good. Here is an example: If you are totally living your life for God and turning away from the evil forces of this world that would make you do bad things, and then someone tries to hurt you or get even with you for something, then this is when this scripture applies to you. God protects those who live for Him, plain and simple! God will not condole our sinful nature.

It would be like you protecting your child against someone bad who is trying to do some serious harm to you child. But if your child was breaking the law or was in some kind of drug deal, what would you do? Or even if your child is down that lost road of no return, and you have tried everything to protect your child from the many dangers of their addictions but can no longer help them, what would you do? What are your choices when you have tried every option and nothing works? Their addiction is just too hard to fight. You cannot protect your child from their own consequences caused by their wrong and deceitful choices that has caused them judgment. The one thing that we as humans cannot run from and that we must face is our own consequences. Now this is similar to how it is with God. God gives us choices, and it is up to each individual to make the right choice. If they choose the wrong choice, then they will suffer their consequences. If God was to save us from our own stupid and selfish mistakes, then no one would ever learn what life is all about. And certainly, no one would ever learn to love or respect anyone. Unfortunately, we have to face the hard-core reality of facing our consequences for our cruel, cold, evil, and selfish ways. And we certainly do not get any rewards or treats for doing something bad. God desires so much to have a lasting fulfilled relationship with you. So, as you meditate on this scripture, here is another one that is really comforting to know.

What shall we then say to these things? If God be for us, who can against us? (Romans 8:31)

This is so awesome to know.

So just remember that as long as you are living for God and someone tries to hurt you or talk evil against you to get you into trouble, wow, just remember God's promise that He is with you and that He will turn what is evil to the good just for you. But please don't misunderstand me. You've got to be living God's ways and not your own human natural ways.

Trust in the Lord with all thine Heart; and lean not on your own understanding. (Proverbs. 3:5)

Note: When it comes to our own understanding, it becomes very limited. Limited decisions make more room for more mistakes.

Here is the definition for the word *condole*!

Condole: to express sympathy with a person who is suffering sorrow, misfortune, or grief.

23

Exchanging Life for Death

My purpose for writing this chapter is based on the cheating way of facing life when reality starts to set in. There is not enough understanding being taught in the world today about what death is and what its purpose is. Because of lack of understanding, people take advantage of death instead of respecting the nature of death itself. So many people are living a life of misery, or should I say hell, because they lack the knowledge of God. Either they refuse to hear about God or they hear about God and don't care, or they just have a different opinion about God. Either way, people's belief system is all messed up, and therefore, they die a miserable death. They are always looking for something or someone to fill their emptiness rather than allowing God in their hearts. It's so sad about so many people dying and going to hell because of disobedience and disbelief. It's very hard for me to bear the pain of knowing what happens to people who do not have a relationship with their one and only creator (God). They would rather exchange their life for death. God gives life to those who seek Him and His promises, but death comes to those who rebel and choose not to follow His ways. Just read this scripture about life and death and what will happen when you choose one or the other: "Death and life are in the power of the tongue; and they that love it shall eat the fruit thereof" (Proverbs 18:21).

The tongue is the most powerful muscle in your body, and I do not mean by physical strength. The tongue has great potential to speak powerful of good or evil words. What you choose to speak will determine the course of your life. But let me remind you that the evil words you choose to speak, you will definitely face the consequences for them. And for those who choose to speak good will enjoy the blessings of it. It all goes with that saying, "Do not do unto others that you would not want done unto you." I am pretty sure you would want people to treat you good and not try to harm you or disrespect you with evil words. So, my friend, choose life and speak good unto others. Let's see what God says about doing unto others (Luke 6:31).

Now here is the kicker: One does not have to be a Christian to live this type of a good life. Someone can be raised by parents that have good standards of living and good morals. But the type of life that God is talking about when God says that life and death are in the power of the tongue, God is insinuating your spiritual life after you have passed away. Now back up for a moment, and let's reflect back on what I meant when I spoke about exchanging life for death and about seeking God. Here is what God says about it in His word: "And ye shall seek me and find me, when ye shall search for me with all your heart" (Jeremiah 29:13).

God is always available, and His longing is that all people will look to Him so they can live a better life. God's arms are always opened to anyone who will turn to Him. But a diligent search is what it will take to find Him, for God wants you wholeheartedly to search for Him. The one who becomes conscious of his need for God, senses the satisfying gift of God, and will set out to find Him can be assured of God's victory. Victory will be yours at the hand of our loving God who delights to welcome His children home. Now that you are aware of these scriptures, please search God with all of your heart. God is so lovable and has so many blessings that He wants to give you when you seek for Him and find Him.

So, remember at the beginning of this chapter, I was talking about exchanging life for death and that it is the cheating way of facing life. Well, the reasoning for that is because many people have no reality of their afterlife and what is to come. But I seriously do believe if people had more knowledge of what to expect when they die, then chances are they would live differently and try to help save others from going to hell. Hell is real, and it is nothing to mess around with, and most of all, people should be afraid of dying and going to hell. But it's so sad because they don't. Though people have many reasons and excuses as to why they cheat themselves out of life, reality just has not hit them.

People choose not to think about reality, and they certainly choose not to accept it. Reality becomes too painful and too difficult to deal with. Reality is the most agonizing and bitter pain because reality is the truth of something that is real. Reality is the hard-core fact of life that we all tend to want to ignore and in hopes that our problem will just go away. Some people are just totally clueless of life and what life has in store for them.

Now in this paragraph, I am about to tell you something about reality that you may not like to read about or that you might not agree with. But please have an open mind when reading this, because you have the right to make the choice to believe what I write or to reject what I write. Thank you. Please continue to read.

It is all about the reality of *life* and how we choose to live it. All too often, people allow themselves to get wrapped around someone else's life. No matter who it is—whether it would be a relationship with your spouse, a relationship with a friend or boss or a coworker, or even just wrapped around the way your parents wants you to be—no matter what the relationship is, it is easy to allow someone else to mold you into their image and to control every aspect of your life. A person's greatest enemy is themselves for allowing it to happen to them. There is no real-world worth living in when you allow yourself to live your life to please someone else. You will be living your life in a constant confused state of mind because people are very hard to please. Life is hard enough to live, then to have to live your life to make someone else happy. In this chaotic world, it is hard enough to make yourself happy, for we cannot change anyone but ourselves! A selfish person is never satisfied; they are always hungry for more of what they have control of, and to allow your whole world to revolve around the one who treats you bad is only your death warrant that you signed. For their hunger and thirst for more will only drain the life out of you. This is one of the reasons why so many people commit suicide. This type of lifestyle can and will push people over the edge of no return for hope. For even all hope has been destroyed.

Now in another way of putting it, many people are mentally too far gone to know what reality is or even to know the meaning of it. In this case, it takes the work of God to help them to know what the meaning of reality is. So many people would rather just live in their own fantasy world. To them, life is easier and does not require much work to operate their meaning of life. They live in a world of make-believe, and when they are called out of that world and forced to face reality, they get scared and try to find the best place to escape. No one likes to leave their comfort zone and face their future of the unknown. And then they will do anything to try and find that comfort spot again so that they can escape reality. Wow, this sums up about how life is, while living in this cold, cruel, and evil world with the "nobody cares" attitude. But whether you believe it or not, God really does care. This is why people's lives are the way they are. Some choose *life,* and some choose *death.* Which one will you choose? I pray that you choose life and turn to God to receive His blessings that He has in store for your life. God really does love you, and He is there for you anytime you decide to come to Him. Just give God that chance to show you how much he loves you.

As I continue speaking about the reality of life, I still do not understand certain parts of my life and what can reality of them parts do to help me to understand more. I am sure there are many parts of your life, if not all of your life, that you do not quite understand and know what the reasoning for it is. This is why I turn to God because He will help me to understand His will for my life, but God does it on His time and terms of condition and not mine. I just have to learn to be more patient with God. And believe me, it will require your full attention and patience from you when you choose to turn to God for all of the answers. Sometimes the choices we make in life are not always beneficial for the way we are living. As a matter of fact, a person can choose to be happy and choose to do the right thing, or they can choose to be miserable and do the wrong thing. It is the same steps with God; you can either choose His ways and live a fulfilled life, or you can choose to live your own ways and try and please everyone who is not happy. That right there is a never-ending cycle and, in return, brings nothing but empty promises, and it will drain the life out of you. Yes, it may sound easy, but in reality, it's not. Now ask yourself this question: Have I ever had any kind of peace, even just a little bit of peace, when I am too busy trying to please other people? Have I ever thought I am just not good enough or there is nothing I can do to please you? You are never satisfied! Have you ever felt drained? Well, there is a reason for all that. People are mere humans, a creature of habits and wants what the body wants and will do anything to get it. The human soul is never satisfied because the soul is always longing for more. Life is so challenging.

People often get caught up in the fact that since their life has important meaning, then they need to live it for others, or either that people are just too busy being selfish that they live life only to please themselves and therefore take advantage of those who do care and try to help. Well, people, for your information, this is called life. But unfortunately, God did not intend for life to be like this; He has a better way with a better plan. But it is your choice to seek Him and find out what his plan for your life is and what way is better for you. Have you ever felt discouraged and disappointed and then wanted to give up because you just cannot seem to find the way to make things work for you? Well, guess what? You are not alone. So why is it that it is so hard to bear the thought of how we treat others when we are thinking of ourselves and the pain that we are in? We are just mere humans and do not often think of other people's pain and the agony that their soul is in, and why? Because it is humanly impossible to endure someone else's pain when we are too busy focusing on ourselves. But can it be done if we live in God's ways? The answer is "yes" because God opens our minds and hearts to love people and see them the way that He does, for nothing is impossible with God. Read Matthew 19:26: "But Jesus beheld them and said unto them, with men this is impossible, but with God all things are possible."

God does not need anything from us to accomplish His plan for our life, but to focus on our human predicament will only paralyze you, because the situation may appear humanly impossible. But you should concentrate on God because His power will help us to see the way out. And right now, you may be unable to see through your troubles and heartaches, but if you stay focused on God and put your trust in Him for the way out, then that is all God needs to begin His work in you. I am sure that you have heard of that saying "Love thy enemy." This is one of God's greatest commands. You say, "Well, how am I supposed to love my enemy when they don't love me?" Good question! It is the work of God in you that makes it possible. There is just no way that any human being can honestly and truly love their enemy by themselves because humans are selfish and cruel, and it is in the human nature to want to hate our enemy instead of loving our enemy, especially if our enemy has brutally did us wrong. What about you? What do you think? Do you think you can honestly, unconditionally love your greatest enemy on your own, basically without the help from God? Just ponder on that question for a while, and then ask yourself, "Why not?" What about if you could love the way that God loves, 2796 but doing it in your own will without God helping you, would you love your enemy? Seriously, what do people really think when they are in that state of mind? My guess is *hate* comes to their mind.

24

Life Is So Precious

Life is just as precious, as it has a purpose. The two go hand in hand with each other, precious and purpose. Don't mistake this chapter from the previous chapter of life's purpose. Take note of what this chapter is about and why it is so precious.

Life! What purpose does it serve? Why is it so precious and very vital and yet people have no clue to the purpose of its existence? And why does it seem like some people have life as if they have it all together and others do not have it together? I have heard that old saying that God dealt them a bad hand. Have you ever felt that way? God does not play with life as if it was a card game! But unfortunately, people seem to take their life and play it like as if it was a game; either you win or you lose. And many do not take their life seriously; instead, they take it for granted. But for whatever reason, it all goes back to having an empty soul. So, if life becomes a game for some people, what would be the name of it? As for me, I would call it a gambler's life, but only because that is what people do when the play with their life! They are gambling for keeps. Their soul is being gambled away, and who is going to keep their soul? God or the devil! What happens when people gamble? They usually lose. And in this case, gambling your life and playing cards with God, you will lose your soul. Now what is more devastating is when people go as far as selling their own soul to the devil just to satisfy their hunger for gambling. God says in His word about selling and buying of your soul: "And that no man might buy or sell, save he that had the mark, or the same name as the beast, or the number of his name" (Revelation.–13:17). Note: Satanic influences, in the case of unbelievers, a man becomes increasingly in the image of the master he chooses. And the two choices of masters are God and Satan. Which master are you choosing to imitate?

I will take these scriptures and go into more of a detailed explanation, for many people don't understand or even know what the mark of the beast is. The mark is 666, a number chosen because it represents man. What this means is that people are followers of Satan and not God. There is a war going on between God and Satan. God has His kingdom, and Satan has His kingdom, and it is up to each individual of which kingdom they choose to follow. This is why I said in the previous chapters, a child of God or the devil's child.

As I continue in this detailed explanation, make sure you have an opened and clear mind to what you are about to read. I would like to advise you that there is some frightening stuff you are about to encounter as you read this. I would also like to advise you to have a Bible in hand as you read and perhaps a commentary to help you better understand.

The book of Revelation is the most devastating book in the Bible. God tells people what they have to look forward to if they choose not to believe in Him and obey His commandments. So let me remind you that if you are not a follower of God, then you will be marked with the number of the beast, 666. But also, I would like to remind you that it is not too late to turn from your evil ways and return back to your first love (God). God loved you first before you were formed in your mother's womb. You also need to know that your life is being operated on a time clock, and your time is running out. Your life, the physical body, does have an expiration date, and unfortunately, you don't know when. Only God knows that time frame.

You may wonder by now what is the mark of the beast and for what purpose does it serve, what does it actually mean? Well, first of all, it is the physical body that will be marked with the numbers 666, either on the forehead or the right hand. The mark will represent that you are a follower of Satan and his evil ways. Satan has bought your soul, and God cannot buy you back from the devil.

Once you sell your soul to the devil, you are his to keep. This mark will identify who you belong to. Now you may wonder how a person can get that mark placed on their body. The mark represents a sold sign. Your soul has been sold! This may seem a bit confusing about how a person can sell their own soul. But God makes it very clear in His word that if you choose not to believe Him and obey His commands and be a follower of His Son, Jesus Christ, then your soul will be sold to the devil. We have a choice of who we will allow to control our life, *God* or *Satan*.

The mark of the beast will be a necessity to buy or sell. The number 666 is used as a barcode to identify who bought your soul. Now the number 666 represents man because the beast will appear as a man.

Here is wisdom. Let him that hath understanding count the number of the beast; for it is the number of men; and his number is six hundred threescore and six. (Revelation 13:18)

Back to the question, how does a person get this mark implanted in them? First of all, it will be a chip about the size of a grain of rice implanted surgically in the forehead or the right hand.

And he causeth all, both small and great, rich and poor, free and bond, to receive a mark in their right hand, or in their foreheads. (Revelation 13:16)

This scripture specifically says the right hand.

As I have mentioned previously in this chapter about the prisons being full of inmates, they are not the only ones who either sell or give their soul to the devil. People make deals with the devil every day. Some acknowledge that they are doing it, and some do not realize that they are. Here are some examples of people who sell their souls to the devil. Prostitutes, they sell their body for money and then pay their pimps. Then there are drug addicts; they make deals for drugs, have sex for drugs, they even steal for drugs—they will do anything it takes to get their next fix. Then you have the gamblers. They will gamble everything they own just to make more money, and in return, they end up in debt.

And in the meantime, the devil is laughing his head off and telling you thank you for serving Him. Then he says, "Come back again!"

Here is something you should also know. I heard this saying, "You only live once, and you only die once." But do not be fooled, my friend, because God says in His word that you live twice and die twice. When a person is born into this world, they are born with a spirit. So, this means that people have a physical life and a physical death, then after your physical death, a person will either have life in the spiritual realm, or they will have what God calls "the second death" (Revelation. 21:8). Note: God mentions several classes of different people who will have a part in the lake that burns with fire and brimstones. All those who remain in their sins will be assigned to the lake of fire as their final destiny. This judgment takes place by God.

Life and death are only a breath away from your final destiny. And both of them are as real as the other. So, remember, how you live your life here on earth will determine your final destiny. Life here on earth is shortly-lived compared to living in eternity. Eternity is forever and ever, and there is no time clock in eternity. Your eternal life will not expire, like your physical life does. Let me rephrase that and make it easier to understand it. Your body has a built-in time clock, and when your time to die is up, your physical body will expire. But your spirit has no time clock; it will continue to exist until you reach your final destiny.

Which is *the second death*?

I hear people talk about life and death like as if it has no meaning. But believe me, my friend, it very much does have meaning and a lot of it. It's time for you to acknowledge the meaning of your life and why you exist. Here is the most important clue: The purpose of your life is only found in Jesus Christ. If you do not know Jesus Christ, then your life has no meaning, and you will be constantly looking for something or someone to fulfill that purpose that is missing in your life. You will be living a worthless and aimlessly life. But why am I being so blunt and rude? Well, because anyone who is living their life in drugs, sex, alcohol, lies, cheating, gambling, etc. to try and find anything of worth and value is worthless and in vain. So, excuse me for being up-front and honest, but it is the truth. And yes, the truth does hurt because no one wants to accept the pain that comes from facing reality Your soul will be in a constant state of emptiness when you choose to live without Jesus Christ and accept God's ways of living your life. God has a plan for your life; He has a plan for everyone. But you need to allow God to take control of your life and let God fill your empty soul instead of trying

to do it yourself. There is nothing in this world that can satisfy your soul. The world has nothing good to offer you but grief and misery.

Now when you have no respect for God or yourself, then you will fail to realize God's purpose for your life. Then eventually, your pain will eat you alive. And if you do not identify what it is that is causing such pain, it will eventually kill you.

25

My Heart's Cry for Prayer

All too often, I think back at my past life and of how I once lived it. I am very thankful that God has rescued me from the pit of hell and showed His mercy for me. I am also very grateful for all the blessings that He has given to me in my life, especially my family. But my heart cries out in agony for my prayers of the lost souls.

There is nothing more agonizing than the sound of lost souls crying out to God for redemption. When people's souls are in pain, they do not often realize the cause of it or don't even know that their soul is in pain. All they know is that they hurt deep down inside from their heart and don't know what to do about it. This is why my heart cries out for prayers of the lost souls. My heart just aches at knowing that there are lost souls out there that are going to hell because they turned their backs on God and then blame God for the bad things that happen in their life.

There is something that I am very curious about. You see, in the Bible, God says that we all will be judged on judgment day, and God said that we all will give an account for the way that we have lived while here on earth. I have read in 2 Corinthians 5:10 that we must appear before Christ, and whether we are good or bad, we will receive the things done in the body, according to what has been done in the body. And 1 Peter 4:5 says that we will give an account to Him, meaning Christ, who is ready to judge both the living and the dead. Then in Romans 14:12, each one of us shall give an account of ourselves to God. And then another one in Matthew 12:36 says for every idle word we speak, we will give an account for, come judgment day. So, what is God saying about the dead? For how can one speak if they are dead? What exactly is God meaning when he talks about the dead? Well, this certainly makes you think about how you are living your life; I know it certainly makes me think about how I am really living and why I am living! But what does *idle* mean? In the *Standard College Dictionary*, it says "unwilling to work, avoiding effort, lazy." Now in the Bible dictionary *Nelson's New Illustrated*, it basically means the same thing: useless, inactive, lazy. So back to the question! What is God's meaning?

Now it makes me wonder what will I say to God about how I have lived my life here on earth, and what about others? I wonder what they will say. For no one can lie to God or make excuses. Will people blame other people for the way they have lived? Or will people blame God for the way they have lived? I know for sure that I will not blame God, because God is the only one who helps me through life's toughest battles, and I know that God loves me. But I also know that there are times when God will cause something bad to happen to me, just so He can bring me up higher to a whole new level. Pain brings change; I will always remember this, for you cannot live life without feeling some type of pain, because life itself is full of pain!

If our body is dead, so are our minds to think and our mouths to speak. Does our spirit talk to God and tell Him what we did or did not do while living in our body on earth? So how does this all work when we are being judged? And here is another question. Does our spirit know what our minds were thinking when we were alive? Does our spirit remember things that our body forgets when it dies? I wished that I totally knew the answer, because it would really make a lot of difference in my life today.

The only thing that is mentioned in the biblical footnotes is that while we are living here on earth in our earthly bodies, what we do with our bodies will be accounted for, and how we use our time will be accounted for. Our most ultimate accountability is to be serving our Lord while we are here on earth. Our life on earth will either make us or break us! We are responsible for our own behaviors, and God will hold us to that responsibility, and God will hold us accountable for those responsibilities!

I also do know that this is very serious, and we need to understand that we will either be rewarded for our good deeds or we lose our rewards. The reward that I want is to hear Jesus Christ say to me, "Faithful and good servant, well done" (Matthew 25:23). This is my dream, and my desire to live a righteous and holy life before God, but I want you to know that I cannot and will not do this on my own. For I know I need God to give me His spirit to remain righteous and holy before Him. For I know that I am nothing without Him (God). And to do this, I need to live a life of love, respect for.

God and others, doing good deeds for God and for others, and to live in holy conduct and godliness. Only God can help me to live this way. This I need to do by keeping watch for Jesus Christ's return and by keeping up with my prayers, especially for my enemies. I will treat my enemies with love and respect just as God treats us! Now when I think about judgment, it is a very scary thought about how I am living and how I am going to be judged. Only God knows the heart of a human being, even more than we do, or think we do! Just because we think that we are being good, doing good does not necessary mean that we are, because our minds can deceive us. All we can do is stay on course with God and ask him to forgive us when we do wrong, then repent of our sins and obey God, for God does give us His assurance that we are forgiven when we confess our sins and repent from them with an honest heart.

Jesus Christ is our only salvation for eternity, and without Him, the lost souls are doomed for hell. These are the hard-core facts. For God's word explains it all in the Holy Bible. So, wake up, people, and start acknowledging the reason for the pain in your soul. If you are still alive, then it is not too late to seek God with all your heart and ask Him for forgiveness of your sins. God has His hands out just waiting for you to come to Him for your rescue. God loves you so much that He sent His one and only Son, Jesus Christ, to die for you so that you can be redeemed and have a beautiful relationship with God. Oh, amen to that. So, what does it mean to live life without God? It means nothing but misery and heartaches, and you will never be at peace, and, of course, your soul will remain with pain. Believe me when I say, this is no life to live.

2981 Each day you wake up, you have choices to make, and you will always learn something from your choices. But what you learn from your choices and how you handle them will determine how you live for your future. You see, to me, life is about learning how to live through all of life's struggles and how to be content in what you have. To me, I believe that I am living life to the fullest when I live for God and to love others as I love myself. And when you pour out your life into the needs of others in God's way, the rewards will come back to you. God promises you that.

So, it is my desire to pray that each given day that you wake up, you will make the right choices and to live for God and seek His ways to live your life to the fullest. Believe me when I say that you will receive His blessings for your life. I promise that it will be the best choice that you will ever make in a lifetime. For God is love.

So may the good Lord bless you as you wake up!

26

Shaping Your Life through Who You Imitate

This chapter is unique due to the fact that not many people realize how their life is being shaped by who they are imitating. People get so caught up in life that they have no time and do not make the time to really look at how they are really living, and to top that off, many people just do not care. They live their life too aimlessly with no sense of direction. I would like for you to open your mind and your heart as you read this chapter and to take a very good look at where your life is headed and ask yourself, "Who am I imitating?" And then ask yourself, "Why am I imitating?" How is your life being impacted by imitating whatever it is or whoever it is that is influencing you? Now when you are finished reading this chapter, go back and read these questions again!

Children! Must I say *children*? Yes! Children's lives are being shaped from the minute they are born! Children have no control or say-so over their life until they become the legal age to make their own decisions. Until then, their lives are being shaped by their parents, their school teachers, their peers, the law, and even strangers. For example, in foster homes, many children are placed in the state's custody and put in foster care because they are removed from an abusive environment that their parents put them in or their parents have passed away, and even more sadly, when they are giving up for adoption. No matter what the situation is, their life is being shaped.

The first five years of the child's life, the parents or foster parents are the ones who influence children the most, and then as the child starts school, they then have their teachers. Then as the child reaches junior high, they start learning from their peers, and then usually by the time they are in high school, their life is pretty much shaped, although there are times when children's lives are shaped by the time they are in junior high. It has been known for younger children, as young as eight years old and up, start getting into alcohol and drugs and then become violent and into gangs. Then eventually they start killing animals and people. It is so sad how a child's life can be damaged at a young age all because of the way their life was shaped. And what is worse is that their life is shaped by others who have the control over them. Children are imitators of those who are shaping their lives.

So, what happens to these children when they turn eighteen and become legal age? Unfortunately, some children do not make it to their eighteenth birthday before they are either in jail or dead. But for those who do reach eighteen, they will continue to live their life as they were taught growing up. History always seems to repeat itself. As they get older, they tend to seek out for people to imitate that reminds them of how they were shaped as a child growing up. The only thing they know is what they were taught. I do believe that empty souls are formed by the way people are being shaped, because if a child grew up without knowing God, then that child's soul is empty, and that child will seek out anything and everything to fill their emptiness. Even children who were raised knowing God can also have an empty soul, because the teachings of Jesus Christ were not the true gospel. Example: a religious cult.

So, who are you imitating? Who are you allowing to shape your life? Are they a good influence or a bad influence? Will you allow them to determine your destiny? Just remember, there is life beyond your grave! It is very important to analyze yourself each and every day to determine who will shape your final destiny. As for me, I am imitating Jesus Christ, and I will allow Him to shape my life and determine my final destiny. Ask yourself, what choices are you making? Look all around you and watch other people and how they act. Everyone is imitating someone and being shaped by someone. But there are so many people being shaped in so many different ways, and so many people are imitating so many other people. Look at your life. Do you see yourself like those other people? This is what crosses my mind when I see how people act. And at times, I find myself acting like other people. But then I stop and think to myself, *Is this how I am supposed to act? Am I imitating Jesus Christ, or am I imitating other people?* For I cannot imitate both. I cannot allow other people to shape my life and choose my final destiny for me. I need to have Jesus Christ to shape me and to determine my final destiny. For Jesus Christ is the lover of my soul, and that I am very proud to have. Thank You, Jesus, for loving me and choosing me to serve you until my final destiny comes.

My dear friend, I ask you to allow Jesus Christ to shape your life and determine your final destiny. God has promised that He will never leave you or forsake you. God wants you to imitate Him and

His Son, Jesus Christ. God's love is greater than any human love possible, and God's love is unconditional. No human can match God's love for humanity.

I hope this book has been an inspiration and a blessing to you. I do hope that you have learned from this book and hopefully applied it to your life. I am very grateful to have the opportunity to write this book, but most of all, I give God all the praise and glory for this book, because I believe it is God who inspired me to write this book.

Thank you.
God bless you.

27

Salvation

What one must do to be saved from the pit of hell!

What needs to be done for someone to get saved from this awful pit of hell? As God says in His word, it is very clear of what must be done! First things first is that one must certainly believe that there is a living God of this universe and that Jesus Christ is the only begotten Son of God. Here are the scriptures.

For God so loved the world, that he gave his only begotten Son, that whosoever believeth in him should not parish, but have ever lasting life. (John 3:16)

And Simon Peter answered and said, Thou art the Christ, the Son of the living God. (Matthew 16:16)

He that believeth and is baptized shall be saved; but he that believeth not shall be damned. (Mark 16:16)

Then Peter said unto them, Repent, and be baptized every one of you in the name of Jesus Christ for the remission of sins, and ye shall receive the gift of the Holy Ghost. (Acts 2:38)

Repent—change of mind, turning from your sins, the concept is that of a complete alteration of the basic motive and direction of one's life, and is often equivalent to conversion. (*The New Concise Dictionary*)

And with many other words did he testify and exhort, saying, Save yourselves from this untoward generation. (Acts 2:40)

So, the very first thing that must be done is for one to believe. You must believe in God and His Son, Jesus Christ, before you can be baptized. Second thing is to repent. As I had mentioned previously about the meaning of repenting, it is not only about turning away from your sins but also about forgiveness of your sins. Each believer that has repented of their sins and has accepted Jesus Christ by faith must receive baptism. Third, now you must be baptized!

As you read about baptism in God's word, baptism is about an individual committing their self fully to serving Jesus Christ. Water baptism signifies that you are a child of God. And the response of baptism to the believer is what Christ has done for all mankind on the cross. Water baptism also portrays the union of the believer with Christ in His death, burial, and resurrection. This signifies an end to a life of sin and a beginning of a new life in Jesus Christ. But as a child born of God, you must remember that water baptism involves a commitment to a lifelong practice of turning away from the world and all of its evil in it and pledging yourself to live a new life in the spirit that reflects God's standards of righteousness.

Now that you are a child of God, it is time for you to start living the benefits that God gives you and understand that God loves you so much that he sacrificed His only Son, Jesus Christ, to save you from going to hell. There is nothing in this world better than living a life with our precious Jesus and to be in His presence and knowing that your future is secured in knowing that you will be in paradise with God when you pass from this life into the next. Please clap your hands and give God praise for what He has done for all mankind.

Thank You, Lord.

Listening to the World or to God

"Dear children, you are from God and have overcome them, because the one who is in you is greater than the one who is in the world" (1 John 4:4). This part talks about the Holy Spirit who lives in you, and He is greater than Satan who is in the world. Nonbelievers are from the world and therefore speak from the viewpoint of the world, and the world listens to them. We are from God (Christians), and whoever knows God listens to us, but whoever is not from God does not listen to us. This is how we recognize the spirit of truth and the spirit of falsehood.

The people you listen to will be the people who shape your life. Listening is a choice based upon what you really want and believe. So, the people of God should listen to Him because they desire Him and His holiness. But many people reject God and our Lord Jesus Christ, preferring the world itself, "feels good" agenda. And so those who desire the world's standards will listen to worldly wisdom and be functionally antichrist, while those who desire the Lord will listen to Him. The people of the world are absorbed with what they can do and get in order to satisfy their worldly desires, and their motivation is essentially pro-self and antichrist. Therefore, they are exactly replicates, the motivation of Satan, whom Jesus described as the person who likes to rule the world (John 12:31). On the other hand, the people who receive the Word of God with gladness (Acts

2:41) are not threatened by all that is antichrist, because Christ is in them, and His Spirit empowers them to stay true to the truth. The world cannot offer anything of lasting value but whoever follows Jesus will live forever (1 John 2:17). Your Spirit will live forever. In the same way that the devil had no hold on Jesus, neither does he have any right to control Jesus's disciples. They do not have to listen to him or his messengers. But worldly people have no problem in rejecting Christ if His way is inconvenient for them or obstructs their desires. And so, the "listening test" (who listens to who) is important to discern those who desire the Lord, and those who do not. Believers find great comfort in knowing that "the One who is in you is greater than the one who is in the world." Despite being surrounded by worldliness, we do not have to accept its messages, and it's important that we do not have to. Instead, we should welcome every voice which speaks truthfully about our Lord Jesus Christ so that we can learn to follow Him better. Meanwhile, we need to be alert to discern the other voices which try to pull us away from our Savior. We must not let them control us or our family, church, or any other area of our lives, because Christ is in us, and we belong to Him.

Prayer: Lord God Almighty, Thank You, that Your voice alone has full authority over everyone and everything everywhere, for all time and eternity. Forgive me for listening to voices which are antichrist and allowing myself and my family to be influenced by the world's agenda because I have failed to discern their origin and motivation. Please, give me the wisdom and the desire I need to choose the messages I listen to, because I love You! In Jesus's name I pray, Amen. Now is the judgment of this world: now shall the prince of this world be cast out. (John 12:31)

Through the cross and resurrection of Jesus Christ, the defeat of Satan and all he stands for has begun. Satan has the power and the authority in this world, and he uses the things of this world against Jesus Christ and His disciples. This is why friendship with the world is enmity with God. This does not mean you cannot be friends with people; it means a Christian believer should not do the things of this world that nonbelievers would do or the former things you did before you became a Christian.

Then they that gladly received his word were baptized: and the same day there were added unto them about three thousand souls. (Acts 2:41)

And the world passeth away, and the lust thereof: but he that doeth the will of God abideth forever. (1 John 2:17)

Most of our life is spent grasping at things to help make us stronger, cure our struggle with habits and addictions, and lead us to a better, more successful life. It's our human desire to feel accepted and loved, and we believe it is in the fixing of ourselves that we achieve all this and finally have the life we've always wanted. But it's not true. Our good God knows a better way.

I found myself in this wanting-to-fix-me place several years ago after tiring of the constant cycle of a roller-coaster Christian life, my fears, my decisions, desire for human value and acceptance that kept me insecure and held me back from things I knew God wanted me to do. I craved anything that might help me and reached for the usual tools: books on the subject of my particular struggle, conversations with a safe friend, pulling the covers back over my head to sleep off my anger, because of the thought I might never be the person both God and I wanted.

I wracked my brain for the times in my life I had felt God the most near, where my greatest spiritual growth had occurred. And I remembered, the only way I found to get better is to focus on God more and not with some legalistic, religious rules and to-do lists but by giving Him (God) my entire heart and strivings, I came back to death to self, the way of the cross. The truth is, my friend, wanting God more than anyone or anything else in our life is the purpose of life. We can try to fix ourselves, but that's doing it our human instincts' way, which won't produce lasting results. When we dive into God's word and stay focused on Him more, then the things of our flesh that we have tried so hard to kill will naturally fall away. Our desire for Him changes everything.

But we don't just arrive there. The flesh is willful, and the pull of the world is strong, and our old habits of trying to fix ourselves die hard. But God, in Him we have a "hope [that] does not disappoint" (Romans. 5:5 NASB), which means that while we are constantly disappointed by our own efforts to get better, focusing on Him to change us is a life guarantee.

Wanting God is a purposeful pursuit. It requires daily focus and will require quality time with Him through prayer and reading of the Bible. Maybe that sounds hard. But living without wanting God brings a difficult life, which most of us have tried and known.

And if we are tired of trying to fix ourselves, we are in the best place we can ever be to start the "wanting God most" journey. It's always in our place of lack that our heart screams out the loudest for God, powerfully brings change.

Now it's your turn.

Roller coasters may be fun at an amusement park, but when it comes to life, most of us are tired of living up and down. Get out a piece of paper, and write down all the ways you've tried to fix yourself through the years. Now write down how wanting God the most would change that. Is it worth doing it His way versus yours? With God, all things are possible. And that, my friend, God made it His promise. See scriptures.

And he said, The things which impossible with men are possibleith God. (Luke 18:27)

But Jesus beheld them, and said unto them, With men this is impossible; but with God all things are possible. (Matthew 19:26)

While trying to understand these scriptures, you must remember that this statement of Jesus must not be taken as an unqualified promise. *All things* do not represent everything we think of. Our prayer of faith must be based on God's will for our life, and we should never ask for anything foolish or things that are wrong. The faith required here must be received as a gift from God. And God will implant that in the hearts of seekers who will lives faithfully according to God's will and purpose for living.

My personal note:

My heart is very saddened to know that there are so many people in this world who know, or at least think, that they are going to hell and yet seem to enjoy it. They think it's some kind of joke, because they have so much anger, confusion, and hatred built up inside of them that their soul just grows numb and their heart turns cold. But in reality, if they really knew and understood what hell was like and had a chance to experience the burning and torture of their soul, would they change their mind and perhaps have a change of heart? Makes me wonder, do you? Many claim to be devil worshippers and seem to like it, but why? Sometimes, life just does not make any sense, and with me being a Christian, living for God and writing this book, even I do not totally understand why life happens the way it does. But I do know that God is in control of everything, and only God knows the hearts of people.

So now, my friends, I hope you have enjoyed reading this book, and most of all, I do hope that you have learned something from it. I hope that you take this book seriously and study the scriptures that are written in this book. Time is a luxury that we do not have. Now is the time to decide who you want to follow in life, *God* or *Satan*. And now is the time to think about where you will spend your eternal destiny.

God bless you, my friend, as you make your choice.

ABOUT THE AUTHOR

Juanita R. Vedder is fifty-five years old. The author is currently attending college for her masters is English. Reading, writing, studying, and researching will always be her life of work. Juanita has a vision impairment that has left her almost totally blind. She is a Christian and spends many hours reading and studying God's word. She loves to write nonfiction and spiritual books.